Cambridge Elements

EARLY MODERN ATLANTIC CITIES

Mariana Dantas
Ohio University
Emma Hart
University of Pennsylvania

Shaftesbury Road, Cambridge CB2 8EA, United Kingdom

One Liberty Plaza, 20th Floor, New York, NY 10006, USA

477 Williamstown Road, Port Melbourne, VIC 3207, Australia

314–321, 3rd Floor, Plot 3, Splendor Forum, Jasola District Centre, New Delhi – 110025, India

103 Penang Road, #05–06/07, Visioncrest Commercial, Singapore 238467

Cambridge University Press is part of Cambridge University Press & Assessment, a department of the University of Cambridge.

We share the University's mission to contribute to society through the pursuit of education, learning and research at the highest international levels of excellence.

www.cambridge.org
Information on this title: www.cambridge.org/9781009468060

DOI: 10.1017/9781108782937

When citing this work, please include a reference to the DOI 10.1017/9781108782937

First published 2024

A catalogue record for this publication is available from the British Library.

ISBN 978-1-009-46806-0 Hardback
ISBN 978-1-108-74954-1 Paperback
ISSN 2632-3206 (online)
ISSN 2632-3192 (print)

Early Modern Atlantic Cities

Elements in Global Urban History

DOI: 10.1017/9781108782937
First published online: March 2024

Mariana Dantas
Ohio University

Emma Hart
University of Pennsylvania

Author for correspondence: Mariana Dantas, dantas@ohio.edu

Abstract: The Atlantic world was an oceanic system circulating goods, people, and ideas that emerged in the late fifteenth and early sixteenth century. European imperialism was its motor, while its character derived from the interactions between peoples indigenous to Europe, the Americas, and Africa. Much of the everyday workings of this oceanic system took place in urban settings. By sustaining the connections between these disparate regions, cities and towns became essential to the transformations that occurred in this early modern era. This Element traces the emergence of the Atlantic city as a site of contact, an agent of colonization, a central node in networks of exchange, and an arena of political contestation. Cities of the Atlantic world operated at the juncture of many of the core processes in a global history of capitalism and of rising social and racial inequality. A source of analogous experiences of division as well as unity, they helped shape the Atlantic world as a coherent geography of analysis.

Keywords: Atlantic world, early modern urban history, colonial encounters, Atlantic revolutions, port cities

ISBNs: 9781009468060 (HB), 9781108749541 (PB), 9781108782937 (OC)
ISSNs: 2632-3206 (online), 2632-3192 (print)

Contents

1 Introduction

In the mid-eighteenth century, Olaudah Equiano was kidnapped from his native African village to be enslaved. "After traveling a considerable time" from the interior of West Africa to the Atlantic Coast, he wrote, "I came to a town called Tinmah," which Gloria Chuku identifies as one of a few towns located, along with Calabar and Bonny, in the Niger Delta.[1] Soon after, he was sold into the Atlantic slave trade. Equiano survived the torments of the Middle Passage on a slave ship to arrive in Bridgetown, Barbados, where he and several other enslaved people awaited their fate while confined in a merchant's yard. During the years he spent in slavery, he was claimed as property by a British naval officer and served at sea during the Seven Years' War (1756–1763). At some point, he was sent to London, "the place I had long desired exceedingly to see," where he recovered from a bout of illness. He later witnessed military action against the French town and fort of Louisbourg, in Nova Scotia. Back in England, he was baptized a Christian in St. Margaret's Church in Westminster, London. Sold to a Montserrat-based merchant in 1763, Equiano worked for three years on commercial ships, trading some of his own wares when he could. During this time, he recounted, he was met with much better treatment in the town of Plymouth, Montserrat, than in Charles Town, South Carolina, or Savannah, Georgia. He had the opportunity to sell some of his goods "at the elegant town of Philadelphia" and to visit ports and markets in towns around the West Indies. He particularly "admired St. Pierre [in Martinique], which is . . . built more like an European town than any I had seen in the West Indies." After purchasing his manumission and becoming free, Equiano continued to rely on his seafaring skills for his livelihood. He then traveled to many more cities around the Atlantic Ocean and the Mediterranean Sea. He found the town of Oporto, in Portugal, to be "well built and pretty, and commands a fine prospect," and in a reference to New York, he declared that he "admired this city very much."[2]

Olaudah Equiano is one of the quintessential figures of the early modern Atlantic world. His memoir, *The Interesting Narrative of the Life of Olaudah Equiano*, narrates his early life in West Africa, his enslavement and forced transportation to the Caribbean and North America, his labors and efforts to acquire his freedom, and his political activism on behalf of enslaved and free Africans and African descendants. The Atlantic Ocean looms large in Equiano's narrative, and throughout his life he crossed it many times. His writings remind us, however, that for all of the activity that took place on ships on oceanic waters, much of the exchange of knowledge, labor, goods, wealth, and so on that marked

[1] Carretta, *Unchained Voices*, 201; Chuku, *The Igbo Intellectual Tradition*, 41.
[2] Caretta, *Unchained Voices*, 235, 236, 250.

the early modern period happened on land and particularly in urban centers. Indeed, Equiano's misfortunes or good luck were often associated with a town or city, or his impending arrival at one.

Starting in the sixteenth century, the world experienced for the first time the global circulation of goods and contact between human populations from all four corners of the globe.[3] Iberian maritime explorations and commercial pursuits, which had begun in earnest in the previous century, integrated Atlantic maritime routes with existing Mediterranean and Indian Ocean ones and markets in Africa and the Americas with those in the Middle East and Asia.[4] Soon after, other European actors, encouraged by the imperial ambitions of the monarchies they served, entered the competition for trading opportunities and colonial possessions. By the beginning of the nineteenth century, all of this activity had transformed the Atlantic Ocean from an uncharted aquatic expanse into a busy place indeed. It had, moreover, globalized commercial networks, consolidated transoceanic empires, and shifted patterns of concentration of wealth and power among peoples of the world.[5]

The historical developments that gave rise to a political-economic system with global reach in which European empires enjoyed primacy unfolded most notably in a network of cities, towns, and villages. Some predated early modern encounters, others formed because of them. These urban sites dotted Atlantic coastal areas and their African, American, and European continental interiors, articulating various linkages between neighboring and distant regions. Port towns facilitated the movement of goods and people across the ocean. Capital cities – some coastal, some inland – housed the governing bodies, merchant communities, and financial agents who dictated the flow of investments and profits. Cities, towns, and villages throughout displayed the material riches and human suffering that Atlantic exchanges produced. They connected urban residents to the world beyond while signaling who might be allowed or not to enjoy its promises.

Overall, urban societies within the emerging Atlantic world varied greatly in form and character. Their environments owed much to local demographic and material realities, economic and cultural practices, and political ties to their hinterland and to other urban centers. Even the designation of a place as a city, town, or village was not historically consistent. Rather, it depended on legal or political urban parameters specific to a certain region or state. Or, in the case of historical descriptions (notably European accounts of African or American

[3] Abu-Lughod, *Before European Hegemony*; Crosby, *The Columbian Exchange*; Pagden, *Lords of All the Worlds*; Russell-Wood, *The Portuguese Empire*, 8–26.

[4] Subrahmanyam, "Introduction."

[5] Klooster, "Introduction"; Chaplin, "The Atlantic Ocean"; Thornton, *A Cultural History of the Atlantic World*, 1–28; Sivasundaram et al., "Introduction: Writing World Oceanic Histories."

societies), it was distorted by the urban expectations of biased observers. As a result, cities, towns, villages, hamlets, forts, or even camps, which were politically, economically, and culturally connected to Atlantic activities, did not share a uniform urban form.[6] They did not have to in order to articulate the exchanges that increasingly defined the early modern era. And therein lies the common element that ties together these different Atlantic urban centers. They were imperial, regional, or local hubs, which housed the institutions and people who mediated encounters between Europe, Africa, and the Americas; funneled material, labor, and financial resources toward oceanic economic pursuits; and facilitated the generation, concentration, and contestation of new forms of wealth and power.[7]

The early modern Atlantic city that we examine in this Element is thus not an archetype but instead a metonym for the urban places where broader historical processes of the early modern era unfolded. Here we focus on three such processes: the encounter between Europe, Africa, and the Americas; the emergence of European empires; and the sociopolitical conflicts that shook societies around the Atlantic, shaping the possibilities and limits of modern freedom. In other words, the Atlantic city spatializes the processes that shaped the first age of globalization just as the global city spatializes globalization in the late twentieth century.[8] Focusing our gaze on these urban places, and sometimes more narrowly on particular urban spaces, illuminates practices and tensions that shaped a recognizable Atlantic past as well as much of our contemporary world.

2 Cities and Atlantic Encounters

During the early modern era, Europeans often indulged in the rhetorical exercise of comparing their capital cities to ancient Rome. Atlantic maritime exploits, commercial expansion, and territorial claims fed dreams of empire and inspired writers and political commentators to invoke the powerful Roman imperial capital in their narratives about Madrid, Seville, London, and others. The comparison with Rome aimed to assert an urban strength and magnificence that was at once the product and generator of empire.[9] "[Y]ou, noble Lisbon, who of all the others in the world, is easily the princess," Luís de Camões wrote in 1572 in *Os Lusíadas*, the epic poem about Portugal's maritime and imperial exploits, "Watch all the heavens determined to make of Lisbon the new Rome."[10]

6 Clark, *The Oxford Handbook of Cities in World History*, 8–13.

7 Nightingale, *Earthopolis*, 155–246.

8 Sassen, "The Global City," 30–32.

9 Bermejo, "Lisbon, New Rome and Emporium."

10 Luís de Camões, *Os Lusíadas*, Canto I: verso 57, Canto VI: verso 7.

If in the late sixteenth century Camões was able to imagine Lisbon rising to the heights of a powerful imperial city, that would not have been the case a century before. At that time, a plurality of urban centers in the Americas, Africa, and Europe served as regional or local centers of power. They articulated networks of material exchange and enforced relationships of political or religious subjugation. Places like Tenochtitlán in Mesoamerica, Cuzco in the Andes, and Gao in the West African interior were imperial capitals (Aztec, Inca, and Songhai empires, respectively). They housed rulers and elites and exercised economic and political control over neighboring peoples. Others, like Teotihuacán, Cajamarca, and Timbuktu (also in Mesoamerica, the Andes, and the West African interior), were religious centers, not necessarily densely inhabited but which enforced regional cultural coherence. A whole ocean separated these African and American urban centers from each other and their European counterparts, preventing urban trends in one continent from affecting developments in another.

That geographic separation had ensured that these cities developed into distinct places. They were built of different materials, laid out in ways that made sense to the people who lived in or transited through them, and served the specific political and economic interests of local elites. Yet they shared some similarities that highlight common human urban developments. Their built environment and everyday activities distinguished them from nearby agropastoral areas in scale, if not in type. Their public spaces and buildings supported communal political, economic, and cultural and religious functions. They congregated people and things while also facilitating their regional dispersion and redistribution. In short, they promoted material, ideological, and cultural ties between regions near and far.

At the dawn of the early modern era, these urban dynamics in the regions that bordered the Atlantic Ocean laid the groundwork for later Atlantic developments. Cities, towns, and villages in Africa, the Americas, and Europe, whether major regional or modest local hubs, served as crucial nodes within well-established networks of exchange. As Europeans ventured into the Atlantic Ocean to establish commercial and political ties between their societies and those on other shores, they relied on urban hubs to command or extend those networks in ways that benefited them. Similarities between non-European and European urban centers informed their decision to establish themselves in or use force to take over a place to access its resources. Differences fed negative biases that helped to justify violent interventions. Indeed, throughout the Atlantic regions, past urban experiences helped different groups of people to make sense of their encounters with each other, to mobilize opportunities, and to mitigate threats. In time, the impact of Atlantic encounters and the expanded urban networks they forged became imprinted in cities themselves, inspiring someone like Camões to imagine his city reigning over all others.

African and American Urban Life at the Dawn of Atlantic Encounters

Urban vitality in Africa and the Americas long predated fifteenth-century Portuguese invasions of North African cities or the arrival of Columbus's fleet in the Caribbean. Rural villages and trading towns housed the population and goods that helped to feed and supply the material and labor needs of surrounding and distant regions. Political and cultural capitals concentrated the wealth, knowledge, and power that enabled ruling elites to assert their influence and prerogatives over sprawling territories. Overall, these were densely inhabited and geographically contained places, marked by complex built landscapes and economic, cultural, and political dynamism. Many changed dramatically or disappeared under the pressures of Atlantic trade and European imperialism. Archaeological and textual evidence reveals, nonetheless, their relevance to evolving political institutions, cultural traditions, and long-distance trade between the fourteenth and sixteenth centuries.

In North and West Africa, different waves of urbanization were related to the expansion of Islam.[11] The organization of an agrarian economy in the first centuries of Islamic state formation was followed closely by the emergence of inland urban centers. From those cities and towns, agricultural production and distribution were organized by ruling dynasties. Some North and West African cities were built over declining ancient urban sites. Others were the result of completely new settlements. Several included features that were common to Islamic cityscapes: houses with large courtyards and small openings onto paved streets; mosques; markets and public baths; and defensive city walls. Their merchant communities and political and intellectual elites helped to cement trans-Saharan networks of exchange that attracted European attention to, and eventual presence in, the region.[12]

The *rihla* (book of travels) of the renowned fourteenth-century Muslim scholar Abu Abdallah ibn Battuta, recorded in 1356, references this important urban network. After many years of traveling throughout the Islamic world, Ibn Battuta undertook a final journey to the kingdom of Mali in 1350–1351. Leaving Fez, the capital city of the Marinid Sultanate (in modern-day Morocco), he crossed the Atlas Mountains southwards to the city of

[11] Monroe, "Elephants for Want of Towns"; Baumanova et al., "Pre-colonial Origins of Urban Spaces in the West African Sahel."

[12] Monroe, "Elephants for Want of Towns"; Boone and Benco, "Islamic Settlement in North Africa."

Sijilmasa, the northernmost point of the Sahara and an important storing location for sub-Saharan goods moving north. After a grueling desert crossing, he stopped in Taghaza, a village he found lacking in every way but that owed its existence to the valuable salt mines in its vicinity (salt being a major regional commodity). Eventually he reached Walata, a provincial Mali capital and home to a well-educated community of Islamic scholars, and finally the Malian capital, which he does not name but was likely Niani. He found particularly notable the capital city's sprawling urbanscape and absence of walls, a testimony to the peace and prosperity achieved by Mali rulers and supported by the region's abundant gold. Ibn Battuta's travels also took him to Timbuktu, then a river port and rising cultural center still of moderate size, and to Gao, an important commercial center in the eastern frontier of Mali. He also stopped in several farming villages in the Mali plains, where trans-Saharan travelers replenished their supplies of provisions.[13]

The importance of these urban centers to the political, commercial, and cultural life of this large section of Africa is also reflected in their inclusion in the Catalan Atlas of 1375, credited to the cartographer Abraham Cresques. The cities of Fez, Sijilmasa, Taghaza, Timbuktu, Gao, and the Mali capital ("Ciutat de Meli") are clearly indicated (Figure 1). The rich exchange of information, as well as goods, that they promoted between Africa and southern Europe ensured their appearance in a map intended to represent the known world at the time.[14] Over the next two centuries, and throughout the early modern era, many of these places remained influential political, commercial, and cultural hubs and central nodes in urban networks that increasingly reached the Atlantic coast. Archaeological evidence of the walls and structures that enclosed these communities signals their development into differentiated, delimited, and regulated spaces.[15] Their material history, moreover, reveals regular contact with Mediterranean and a few Atlantic port cities, foreshadowing an eventual trade in goods and enslaved people with European merchants and empires.[16]

In the region that corresponds to modern-day Nigeria, notably among the Hausa and the Yoruba, Ile-Ife, Benin City, and Kumasi (capital of the Ashanti) became important economic and political centers between the sixteenth and eighteenth centuries. With varying degrees of prominence, these cities helped to articulate regional trade networks that tied their economy to activities along the trans-Saharan trade routes. Their prosperity and the pull effect they exerted regionally were reflected in the palaces, elite residences, and temples and other

[13] Dunn, *The Adventures of Ibn Battuta*, 295–306.
[14] Vagnon, "Pluricultural Sources of the Catalan Atlas."
[15] Connah, "Contained Communities in Tropical Africa."
[16] Monroe, "Urbanism on West Africa's Slave Coast."

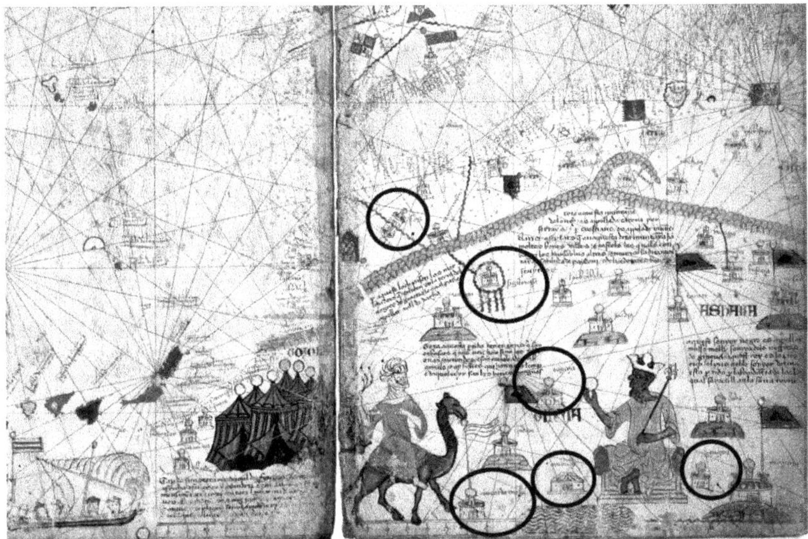

Figure 1 Section of the Catalan Atlas highlighting North and West African cities (1375).

Image prepared by the authors. A digitized copy of the complete Catalan map is available at https://gallica.bnf.fr/ark:/12148/btv1b55002481n.

sacred religious sites they boasted. Within their often walled borders, they concentrated political and military leaders, religious scholars, merchants, and skilled artisans.[17] The relevance of these cities as sites of power, from where regional states exercised their authority, attracted the attention of European traders. Those who visited them reported on the size of their populations, the organization of their public spaces, and the elaborate decorations of their buildings.[18]

The formation and permanence of African cities was related to more than commercial and economic factors and state politics, however. The Yoruba city of Ile-Ife, in modern-day Nigeria, and the capitals of the Mali and later Songhai empires had particular religious and cultural significance. Home to Yoruba and Muslim religious leaders, these cities were also the sites of legendary, divine, or mystical events at the core of shared religious beliefs.[19] Similarly, Mbanza Kongo, the political capital of the kingdom of Kongo in Central West Africa, was home to religious personages around the time of the region's first encounters with Portuguese merchants. The city was an ancestral site for many regional lineages and communities and connected to key events in the region's political

[17] Olukoju, "Nigerian Cities in Historical Perspective," 11–22.

[18] Freund, *The African City*, 1–36. [19] Winters, "The Urban Systems of Medieval Mali."

development. Consequently, it remained continuously inhabited throughout the early modern period.[20] Portuguese urban and material elements were added to the cityscape after the sixteenth century. Mbanza Kongo rulers of that era promoted the use of stone, rather than wood and thatched grass, and a European-Christian style of construction to impress visitors and their subjects. Nevertheless, it was the city's relevance as a site of memory and spiritual power that ensured its longevity amid a period marked by political and military conflict.[21]

The history of African cities at the beginning of the early modern era reveals a rich urban tradition tied to state formation, trade, and consolidation of cultural communities. Fifteenth-century European travelers, however, did not always appreciate the relevance of African cities and towns. Comparing the sites he visited in Senegambia in the 1450s to European cities, the Venetian merchant and member of a Portuguese commercial delegation Alvise Cá da Mosto found the former wanting. He interpreted grass-covered huts and the absence of stone walls as signs of the political and economic shortcomings of local rulers who failed to create, in his view, real cities.[22] His prejudiced assessment of African cities notwithstanding, these urban places helped to sustain institutional and everyday practices that would eventually inform African interactions with Europeans and facilitate the latter's access to African goods and people. Moreover, as people from Africa were enslaved and trafficked across the Atlantic, they carried with them knowledge of cities and towns as places of trade, political engagement, and cultural meaning. Their urban experiences helped them make sense of their new transatlantic reality and of the places they were forced to inhabit.

In the Americas, villages, towns, and cities also helped to organize population settlement, power relationships between different peoples, and networks of material and cultural exchange. Taíno and Tupinambá villages contained differentiated housing that denoted local social and political hierarchies and public spaces for communal activities. Urban centers in the Aztec and Inca empires were home to palaces, temples, and markets where imperial resources and subjects converged and from where ruling elites dispensed material favors and justice. These urban sites additionally played an important role in mediating first encounters and impressions between Europeans and Indigenous Americans. Indigenous Caribbean and South American villages, for instance, attracted the attention of early Iberian explorers and settlers who viewed them as sources of provisions, military allies, and enslaved workers. Mesoamerican and

[20] Thornton, "Mbanza Kongo/São Salvador." [21] Ibid., 68–72.

[22] Bennett, *African Kings and Black Slaves*, 110–121.

Andean towns and capital cities, with more complex and richer built environments, held the promise of even greater colonial wealth.

Indigenous villages in the Caribbean and the mainland Americas were modest in size and construction, as attested by sixteenth- and seventeenth-century European accounts and archaeological findings. The wooden houses, with pleasant-smelling thatched roofs and decorative lattice work, of the Taíno villages of Hispaniola nevertheless impressed the Dominican priest Bartolomé de las Casas. The German explorer Hans Staden also appreciated the Indigenous huts in the Tupinambá village where he was held captive and learned to distinguish the social status of their dwellers by their structural differences. Both men, along with the French Huguenot Jean de Léry, further wrote about the public spaces, which they described as squares or plazas, where villagers held games, ceremonies, and festivities crucial to cementing communal life.[23] Specialized buildings and public spaces were also observed in the eastern seaboard of North America. According to Thomas Harriot's *Brief and True Report* of Virginia, these places had rich gardens between scattered houses and were encircled by palisades, which served to demarcate communal lands more than provide protection.[24]

The Taíno, Tupinambá, and Powhatan villages of the Caribbean, southeastern Brazil, and northeastern America, respectively, provided shelter, sustenance, and community to Indigenous peoples. Under the guidance of their political and religious leaders, moreover, they promoted economic and military practices that ensured their regional survival. Early European settlers sought trade or political relationships with these villages to secure their own material survival and security in these foreign and often hostile lands. Early European writings about these places, though admiring at times, were nonetheless prone to note what they lacked. One chronicler of sixteenth-century Brazil, for example, claimed erroneously that because the Tupi language did not have the letters F, L, and R, the Tupi people had no faith, no law, and no ruler. His comment reveals an inability to recognize a religious, legal, and political culture that others had already recorded. The noted absence of European-styled temples, courthouses, and palaces in European descriptions of Indigenous villages likely influenced such prejudiced views as well.[25]

[23] Badillo, "Guadalupe: Caribe o Taína?," 40; Deagan and Cruxent, *Columbus's Outpost*, 33–34; Fair et al., *Hans Staden's True History*; Léry, *Histoire d'un voyage*, 76.

[24] Harriot, *A Brief and True Report*; Milner, "Palisaded Settlements in Prehistoric Eastern North America."

[25] Deagan and Cruxent, *Columbus's Outpost*, 23–46; Metcalf, *Go-Betweens*, 55–88; Fair et al., *Hans Staden's True History*, xxv–xxxi.

Mesoamerican and Andean towns and cities stood in contrast to these Indigenous villages. They were home to large populations, in the range of tens of thousands of people. Their buildings and public spaces were made of sturdier and more permanent materials, while their political and cultural influence stretched over continental distances. These cities, moreover, were heirs to a strong urban tradition that dated back centuries. Teotihuacán, in the Valley of Mexico, and Tiwanaku, near Lake Titicaca in western Bolivia, for instance, concentrated around 100,000 people at the height of their development during the first millennium CE. Their importance as political and religious centers was such that they informed the urban layout and architectural style of later Mesoamerican and Andean cities.[26] Their ruins, moreover, were eventually celebrated as heritage sites by Aztec and Inca rulers eager to claim territorial belonging and dominance.[27]

The Aztec capital city of Tenochtitlán, whose wealth and monumental constructions so impressed the Spanish, was built to invoke the majesty of Teotihuacán and assert the dominance of the Mexica over neighboring cities and tributary peoples.[28] Comparing it to urban Iberia, the Spanish conquistador Hernán Cortés wrote that Tenochtitlán was larger than Seville. Its people, he noted, lived much like those in Spain thanks to the city's wide streets, aqueducts, large temples and palaces, well-supplied markets, and industrious artisans.[29] A map-view of Tenochtitlán attributed to Cortés and published with his letters in 1524 illustrated these favorable impressions of the Aztec city (Figure 2).[30] Other Mesoamerican and Yucatán cities, while not as rich or monumental, also offered their residents urban amenities and cultural vibrancy that similarly inspired Spanish admiration.[31]

In the Andean region of South America, the ebb and flow of urbanization was connected to the challenges imposed by the natural environment and regional politics. During times of environmental stress or war, rural peasant populations were drawn to cities and towns. These urban centers offered the conditions for their collective survival even if urban ruling elites demanded their political subjugation and labor tribute.[32] During periods of political stability and relative peace, conversely, Andean cities functioned mostly as centers for the collection

[26] Davenport and Golden, "Landscapes, Lordships, and Sovereignty."
[27] Kolata, *The Tiwanaku*, 97–176; Heyden, "From Teotihuacan to Tenochtitlan."
[28] Joyce, "Theorizing Urbanism in Ancient Mesoamerica"; Smith, "Cities in the Aztec Empire."
[29] Cortés, *Five Letter*, 87–94. [30] Kagan, *Urban Images*, 64–65.
[31] Davenport and Golden, "Landscapes, Lordships, and Sovereignty," 204–205. Pedro de Alvarado, one of the Spanish captains on Cortés's expedition, wrote in his letters about well-built towns and cities in Guatemala. Restall and Asselbergs, *Invading Guatemala*, 23–48.
[32] Valdez, "From Rural to Urban."

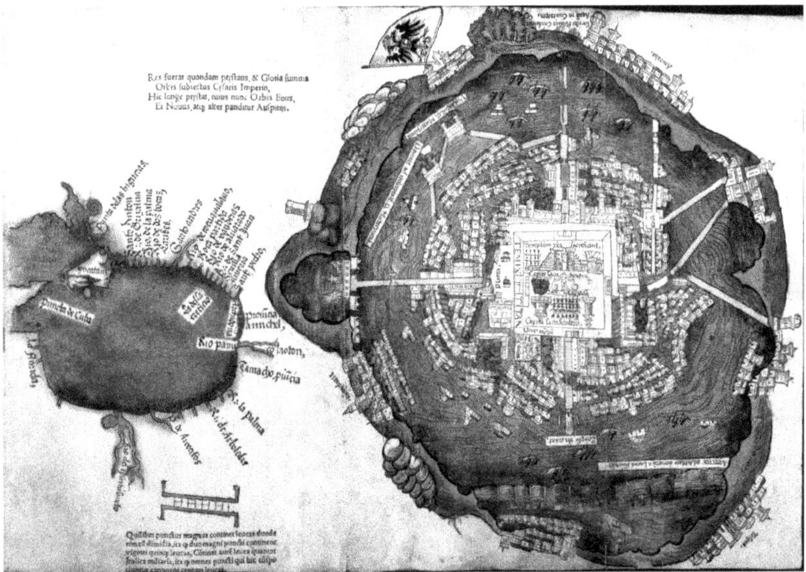

Figure 2 *La Gran Ciudad de Temixiitan* (Tenochtitlán, 1524).
"Cortés' 1524 Map of Tenochtitlan," in *Praeclara Ferdinadi Cortesii de Noua maris Oceani Hyspania narratio* . . . (Nuremberg: Friedrich Paypus, 1524). Newberry Library: Ayer 655.51.C8 1524d.

and redistribution of goods within their networks of rural and subsidiary urban communities.[33]

At the height of the Inca empire, for example, peaceful conditions made it safe for populations to move away from cities. Indeed, like other Andean societies before them, the Inca promoted the colonization of areas in different climatic zones to sustain a diversified economic production and resilient supply network. Imperial authorities then organized an economic system of distribution of goods predicated on political notions of reciprocal obligation. Cities, including the Inca capital Cuzco, served as nodes within this network of exchange. Their built environment comprised buildings that invoked the spiritual and temporal power of ruling elites and large warehouses and squares where the empire's material wealth was collected, stored, and later redistributed during political and religious celebrations. The urban plan and architecture of Inca cities reproduced, moreover, those of Cuzco to create a shared spatial experience that extended Inca territorial claims and cultural hegemony wide and far.[34]

[33] Hagen and Morris, *The Cities of the Ancient Andes*; Vogel et al., *The Casma City of El Purgatorio*.

[34] Kolata, "Mimesis and Monumentalism in Native Andean Cities"; Christie, "The Inka Capital Cusco."

The imposing buildings, spacious squares, and well-provisioned storehouses of the Inca city were often admired by the Spanish, who were nevertheless puzzled by their sparse number of inhabitants and the shortage of male heads of household. Famously, and to the horror of Inca leaders, Spanish conquistadors abused the female population residing in these places and looted reserves of food and other goods. They often lamented, moreover, the location of these cities up in the Andean mountains, which though convenient for Inca purposes, was far removed from coastal areas and potential ports.[35]

Beginning in the fifteenth century, the movement of Europeans southward and westward into the Atlantic thrust the populations of three different continents into contact with each other. As these groups tried to make sense of the opportunities and threats generated by these encounters, they often relied on existing urban resources and their own urban experiences. American and African urban places at the center of networks of material exchange and political systems often proved useful to European pursuits of trading goods and regional dominance. Conversely, the foreignness of African and American cities, towns, and villages, as far as Europeans were concerned, clouded European understandings of Indigenous claims to land, resources, and political power.[36]

European Towns, Ports, Forts, and Factories

European cities, which in time would support Atlantic exchanges, were, much like African and American cities, the product of a centuries-old urban history. In Europe, as in the two other continents, towns and cities developed as centers for the convergence, distribution, and production of various foodstuffs and manufactured goods. The military defense and material survival they guaranteed attracted demographically dense urban populations. They survived over time because of the resources they mobilized, the networks they fed into, and their religious and cultural significance to thousands of individuals.

In contrast to the Americas and Africa, where mostly inland urban centers supported land-based networks of exchange, Europe had several important seafaring cities. Many of those cities later became crucial to the maritime trade that shaped the Atlantic as a connective space thanks to their long-operating ports and dynamic merchant communities. They supported, moreover, efforts by European rulers, elites, merchants, and navigators to establish fortifications and factories (trading posts) on the Atlantic coast of Africa and of the Americas. The strong ties between these outposts and European cities ensured the reproduction of European urban dynamics and landscapes in overseas sites even as they adapted by

[35] Mumford, *Vertical Empire*, 13–40. [36] Chakravarti, "Invisible Cities."

necessity to local material, social, and cultural realities. European ports, forts, and factories became at once by-products of old urban practices and of new maritime exploits. In time, they formed the nodes that connected emergent networks of exchanges in the early Atlantic world.[37]

At the start of the second millennium CE, Europe experienced a period of marked urban growth despite demographic fluctuations. Some cities and towns were the product of continued occupation of Roman urban centers, others of the formation of urban communities along trade routes and near castles or monasteries. In Iberia and Southern Europe, some urban centers emerged as Islamic political and cultural capitals, others in response to Christian rulers' efforts to eradicate Muslim enclaves. In general, cities and towns were the site of markets and fairs that helped to commercialize an expanding agricultural production. They were thus usually well integrated into their hinterland, benefiting the financial interests of landowning elites while also feeding supply networks that supported the daily life of surrounding populations. As these networks of commercial exchange extended further, coastal areas witnessed the revival of old port towns and the formation of new ones. From these locations, goods and credit moved along maritime routes to multiple urban centers, incentivizing the evolution of shipping practices and technology that could support long-distance trade.[38]

Late medieval and early modern European cities and towns were also key to the development of new forms of political alliances between members of these communities and local or regional lords. Secular and religious land holders, eager to encourage the pursuits of merchants, artisans, and others who sustained successful local economies, were willing to grant rights and political autonomy to urban communities within their sphere of authority. Aristocratic and ecclesiastical lords also supported and promoted the establishment of urban settlements with the goal of extending their political power over new territory. In such cases, urban centers helped to defend the territorial claims, political rule, and cultural supremacy of certain elites. In return, segments of these urban populations secured social distinction, economic privileges, and political autonomy through charters, constitutions, and grants. The rights and freedoms town and city dwellers enjoyed as a result of their economic and political relationship with landed potentates gradually became a feature of urban life. Indeed, they became ingrained in Europeans' imagination and understanding of cities and were jealously guarded by urban residents.[39]

---

[37] Parker, "The Artillery Fortress"; Clark, *European Cities and Towns*, 46–49; Miranda, "Before the Empire"; Sicking, "The Medieval Origin of the Factory."

[38] Boone, "Medieval Europe"; Calabi, "Early Modern Port Cities."

[39] Boone, "Medieval Europe," 231–236; Meraglia et al., "How Merchant Towns Shaped Parliaments"; Asenjo-González et al., "Town and Country."

The connection between urban settlements, the incorporation of towns and cities, and territorial and political conquest is evident in the Iberian Peninsula in the context of the reconquista. During the late medieval period, Iberian kingdoms sought control over southern portions of the peninsula under Arab-Islamic rule. Though these campaigns were not exactly a reconquest of previously held territory, the stated goal of "reconquering" the region for Christendom secured papal support and juridical legitimacy for the ensuing wars. An important ally in that effort were members of the lower aristocracy and commoners who rightfully foresaw an opportunity to access land, military distinction, and social and political influence. Political-military leaders thus extended to the willing residents of new urban settlements on the Christian Iberian frontier rights to landed property, tax privileges, and to the formation of local governing councils. Urban residents, in turn, had to establish standing militias and provide military defense. Some towns developed specialized manufactures. Most pursued agriculture within their immediate hinterland. The newly formed urban elites in these towns, whose power was based on land ownership, appointment to governing councils, and military distinction, became crucial supporters of royal authorities and staunch defenders of their privileged status as citizens.[40]

Other European regions witnessed similar connections between the political and territorial ambitions of secular or ecclesiastical authorities and town formation. In the twelfth and thirteenth centuries, Norman and English lords employed urbanization as a tool of territorial and political expansion in Wales and Ireland. The notion that civilization was tied to the urban spatial form and to urban political and socioeconomic organization fed perceptions of Wales and Ireland as uncivilized. The presumed lack of towns in those regions helped the architects of this early colonial project to justify their encroachment. Newly chartered English towns, moreover, granted the invaders legal rights, as well as land and commercial claims, that were not extended to indigenous populations. These privileges strengthened urban settlers' commitment to the expansionist project of Anglo-Norman ruling elites and the political ties between them. Meanwhile, the towns themselves cemented a view of local nonurban indigenous populations as political and cultural outsiders – a reality that foreshadowed later colonial dynamics in the Americas.[41]

The French southwest under the rule of the Counts of Toulouse witnessed its own late medieval wave of newly chartered towns, urbanization, and construction of fortifications. Here, too, landed elites used the spatial and political

[40] Lay, *The Reconquest Kings of Portugal*, 42, 106–107, 143–170; Asenjo-González et al., "Town and Country," 10–17; Maser, "Conquered Cities."

[41] Lilley, "Urban Landscapes and the Cultural Politics of Territorial Control"; Lilley, "'Non urbe, non vico, non castris'."

organization of towns to promote trade. They then demanded part of the wealth urban residents generated in exchange for promises of protection, rights, and socioeconomic opportunities.[42] In late medieval Iberia, England, and France, as well as elsewhere in Europe, urbanization thus helped established or emergent political authorities to capitalize on the economic, political, and social ambitions of local communities. In that context, the improved economic opportunities, political autonomy, and pathways to social distinction offered by urban institutions secured the support of residents of towns and cities for the territorial, monetary, and commercial pursuits of ruling elites.[43]

An important feature of many late medieval and early modern European towns was the urban enclosure or *enceinte*, the walls and fortifications that protected urban dwellers and their economic resources from potential outside threats. Because towns and cities were instruments of control over territory and economic resources, they often found themselves the targets of attacks by political, religious, and economic rivals. Urban communities and their rulers thus reconciled their misgivings about the spatial limitation and financial burdens imposed by fortifications with the need to defend lives and property. Investment in, and military and technological updates of, these urban structures intensified in times of conflict as much as they waned in times of peace. In the centuries leading to and immediately following European Atlantic expansionism, walls and fortifications reshaped the architectural landscape, spatial organization, and urban–rural relationship of European towns and cities.[44] They also informed patterns of early European overseas settlement around the Atlantic.

While some European cities built fortifications, others, involved in an expanding trade between kingdoms and countries, sought to accommodate foreign merchant communities in trading outposts or factories. From these enclaves, commercial agents built important relationships with local figures and urban institutions despite being cultural and political outsiders. They secured, in this manner, the legal right to live, trade, hold property, and conduct business in various cities and towns. Their efforts built strong urban trade networks throughout coastal European regions, sometimes reaching far into the interior of the continent. Their businesses created stable and profitable lines of supply and earned them financial support and privileged status from local economic and political elites.[45] Portugal's main port cities of Lisbon and Porto, for instance, fully benefited from this entanglement between merchant communities, trans-regional commercial networks, urban economies, and elite interests. But when the Hundred Years' War threatened Portuguese merchants'

[42] Barrett, "Origins of the French Bastides." [43] Boone, "Medieval Europe," 226–228.

[44] Tracy, *City Walls*, 88–116, 317–348; Parrott, "The Utility of Fortifications."

[45] Caracausi, *Commercial Networks and European Cities*, 65–186.

activities in the port cities of England, Flanders, Zeeland, and Normandy, they set their sights on North African cities in hopes of accessing new trade networks, markets, and commodities.[46]

Different European merchant communities had long been aware of the promises of intercontinental trade with North Africa and the Levant and the limits of their position within that commercial system. By the fifteenth century, it was mainly Genoa and Venice who held trading outposts in port cities within those regions. Portuguese merchants, supported by a royal dynasty eager to maintain the loyalty of a military noble class and of urban communities, aimed to establish their own. Together these groups organized the takeover of the port city of Ceuta, believing it to be the ideal launching point for a Portuguese expansionist campaign in Muslim North Africa. The Portuguese king, nobility, merchants, urban elites, and even peasants hoped this effort would propel Portugal from its peripheral position to a central economic role in the Mediterranean with gains for all involved.[47]

While Ceuta succumbed to Portuguese attacks and territorial claims quickly in 1415, political control over the city and its hinterland proved much harder to achieve. The Portuguese followed their campaign in Ceuta with the occupation of various other sites on the Moroccan coast. Their efforts in the region were repeatedly thwarted, however, by local dynasties and sultanates. Availing themselves of local material resources and the built environment, the Portuguese worked to fortify their outposts. They also sought to forge political alliances with local populations by extending them military protection and certain urban privileges. Ultimately, however, the project was too costly for the Portuguese crown to maintain. It required continuous military presence and resources without offering the financial returns and hegemonic power it had promised. Portuguese exploits along the sub-Saharan coast, Indian Ocean, and eventually South America redirected, moreover, the attention and interests of the nobility, urban elites, and merchants toward other shores.

By the second half of the sixteenth century, only three Portuguese holdings remained in Morocco. Two centuries later, the last Portuguese city standing in the region, Mazagan, faced the unprecedented experience of being transplanted to the Brazilian Amazonia by the Portuguese imperial state. Its longevity had relied on the presence of a defensive fort, updated and reinforced over the years, within which the town had managed to survive. But persistent local attacks finally convinced the king to use the town to secure the more strategic Amazonian region, where the Spanish and other European empires threatened

[46] Arnold, "Central Europe and the Portuguese"; Miranda, "Before the Empire."

[47] Newitt, *A History of Portuguese Overseas Expansion*, 1–33.

Portuguese territorial claims.[48] Portugal's urban experiment in Morocco had been riddled with challenges and was ultimately abandoned. It set, nevertheless, certain patterns for other European exploits in the Atlantic: the search for urban sites to house a trading outpost or factory; the investment in fortifications; and the pursuit of local alliances through, in part, the extension of urban protections and privileges to native communities.

Portuguese maritime and commercial exploits along coastal West Africa during the fifteenth and sixteenth centuries thus embraced the construction of fortifications. However, instead of conquest, Portugal favored military alliances and an economic and political partnership with local rulers. Rather than attempting another territorial takeover, the Portuguese sought to reproduce the factory system used in European port cities. The absence of large urban settlements on the West African Coast compelled the Portuguese and other merchant communities to set up forts to protect their outposts, primarily from attacks by other Europeans. That was the case with the castle of Saint Jorge of Elmina, built by the Portuguese in present-day Ghana and considered to be the first uniquely European building erected overseas in the context of Atlantic expansionism. As violent European rivalries continued to shape the Atlantic into a contested space, forts were erected to protect Portuguese settlements on the Atlantic islands, in Central Africa, and later in Brazil. Other Europeans adopted the same strategy in Africa, the Caribbean, and the Americas.[49]

The Spanish avidly embraced fortified settlements during their early imperial expansion in the Caribbean and the American mainland. Between 1509 and 1569, the crown ordered the construction of more than 100 fortifications to protect the lives and economic activities of early settlers and to mark and defend territorial claims.[50] These efforts proved justified when colonial Spanish-American coastal ports and towns were repeatedly targeted by rival European agents eager to loot and to undermine Spain's claims of exclusivity to the Western Hemisphere. Fortified trading posts and settlements were also the product of Spanish campaigns into the interior of North America, where *presidios* (military garrisons) and walled religious missions eventually dotted the landscape. Within and along those walls, settler communities and allied Indigenous populations formed towns that in time helped to sustain trade and cultural exchanges, as well as Spain's tenuous political claim to its continental American empire.[51]

---

48 Elbl, "Portuguese Urban Fortifications in Morocco"; Vidal, *Mazagão*.

49 Parker, "The Artillery Fortress"; DeCorse, *An Archaeology of Elmina*, 7–44; Newitt, *A History of Portuguese Overseas Expansion*, 41–53; Leite, "Defender Almas e Corpos nos Açores."

50 Parker, "The Artillery Fortress," 400.

51 Moorhead, *The Presidio*, 3–27; Bense, "Introduction: Presidios of the North American Spanish Borderlands"; Deagan, "Strategies of Adjustment: Spanish Defense," 17–20.

Following in the footsteps of Iberian colonial agents, other Europeans also relied on fortified trading outposts and settlements to establish their commercial, economic, and political presence in Africa and the Americas. Relative latecomers to Atlantic maritime and commercial ventures, the Dutch, English, and French sometimes opted for attacking and overtaking existing Iberian sites. The role these locations came to play in local and regional economic systems made them too attractive to overlook. That was the fate of various Portuguese West African forts and of Spanish sites in the Caribbean and in North America. Throughout the Americas, fortified settlements were also meant to protect trading posts and vulnerable communities from attacks by native peoples, though not all were successful in doing so. But while the construction of these sites was occasionally met with suspicion and hostility, they were sometimes perceived as useful and even welcomed by Indigenous populations. European fortifications, after all, could provide defense and support trade for local Indigenous communities in the same way that they did for European settlers.[52]

European forts and fortified trading outposts, whether complex in design or not, enclosed by stone walls or wooden palisades, helped to advance European colonialism in the Americas. They facilitated trade and diplomatic negotiations, offered refuge, and promoted social and cultural exchanges. Some developed into key Atlantic port towns and political and economic centers despite their often transient resident population thanks to continued European imperial investments.[53] Male residents of overseas forts and towns advanced European rulers' goals of territorial possession, economic gain, and cultural hegemony. In return, they negotiated privileges and degrees of self-government. Attaining these rights through charters, land grants, or political incorporation gave these urban settler communities a sense of legitimacy that emboldened them to claim control over native peoples, lands, and resources. In the process, they helped to cement European imperial reach and power across the Atlantic. Urbanization had proved a useful tool of territorial conquest and assertion of political rule in late medieval and early modern Europe. It would do the same for European monarchies and economic elites in the Americas and to a lesser extent Africa during the early modern period.[54]

Urban Imperial Beginnings in the Atlantic World

As the main population crisscrossing the Atlantic in the first decades of the early modern era, Europeans anxiously sought ways to control their interactions with other groups of people. They built forts on the Gold Coast of Africa, in the

52 Klingelhofer, *First Forts*, 41–64, 85–104, 139–166, 189–208.

53 Reis, *Imagens de Vilas e Cidades*; Boehm and Corey, *America's Urban History*, 42–65.

54 McAlister, *Spain and Portugal in the New World*, 133–152; Hornsby, *British Atlantic, American Frontier*, 180–187; Altman, "Key to the Indies"; Asenjo-González et al., "Town and Country."

Caribbean, and elsewhere, from where they tried to impose their priorities. They used cities, towns, and villages, moreover, some of which they founded, others which they integrated, to cement and diffuse the spatial reach of their overseas power. In West and Central Africa, urban communities remained almost exclusively under the control of African rulers and institutions throughout the early modern era. And yet, villages and towns along the Atlantic coast, whose economy and society became incrementally tied to the Atlantic trade, helped to consolidate European commercial interests. In the Americas, emboldened by long-standing idealizations of the city as a marker and tool of civilization, Europeans' urbanizing efforts were part of an aggressive project to transform indigenous landscapes into colonial spaces. Urban charters, buildings, streets, and markets compelled resident and transient urban populations to interact with each other under the rubric of European laws and practices. All around the Atlantic basin, urban centers mediated Atlantic commercial and cultural exchanges, making room in the process for European demands and prerogatives.[55]

The trajectory of urban settlements in West and Central Africa illuminates the varying influence of Atlantic encounters on the region's towns and cities. Between the fifteenth and eighteenth centuries, European presence in Africa was mostly limited to forts and factories. These sites supported commercial relationships between European merchants, chartered companies, and royal agents, as well as local African traders and political elites. From these places, goods and the enslaved people who generated so much wealth for European empires were shipped across the Atlantic. Their spatial organization, architecture, material makeup, and high concentration of people reproduced elements of European urban culture on the African coast. In time, those elements spilled out from the confines of forts or trading compounds to neighboring villages and towns, changing local habits and encouraging exchanges of a more intimate nature between foreigners and natives. That process is well documented in the villages and towns of the Gold Coast (Figure 3), Bight of Benin, and Bight of Biafra. The strength of indigenous African communities prevented European territorial or political incursion. Still, the activities and exchanges facilitated by these places enabled European imperial expansionism and helped to cement white dominance and wealth in the Atlantic world.[56]

European presence on African shores influenced the trajectory of urban life in West Africa in other ways, with its impact changing over the course of the early modern period. Early Atlantic trade encouraged the growth and expansion of

[55] Santos, "Luanda: A Colonial City"; Candido, *An African Slaving Port*, 44–67; Saupin, "Emergence of Port Towns."

[56] Ipsen, *Daughter of the Trade*; Law, *Ouidah*; Sparks, *Where the Negroes Are Masters*.

Figure 3 Sketch of the Castle of Elmina and the neighboring Fante town (1731–1732).

Robert Durand, May 31, 1732 to September 3, 1732, *Journal de bord d'un negrier: Guinée*, p. 39, Beinecke Rare Books and Manuscript Library. https://collections.library.yale.edu/catalog/2007542.

networks of villages and towns that fed coastal trade. Portuguese demand for gold, cloth, and other commodities used in the Indian Ocean trade, for instance, incentivized the concentration of miners, artisans, and merchants in urban settlements along trade routes linking the West African hinterland to the coast. As rival European merchants established themselves in the region, increasing demands for trading goods, the system of villages that supplied this coastal trade expanded. Some urban populations increased to tens of thousands of people and European visitors described the cities they encountered as large, well-organized, and richly appointed.[57] However, as the trade in enslaved people dominated Africa's commercial dealings with Europe, that urban pattern shifted. Villages became less relevant as sites of production of material commodities and were often targeted as sources of commodifiable humans. As those communities dwindled, their enslaved members who were not destined to the Middle Passage and chattel slavery in the Americas remained in capital cities and coastal ports. Their numbers enlarged those urban populations while their labor animated the economy in those places.[58]

The Atlantic slave trade also affected the economic underpinning of West African urban politics. Capital cities that were located in the interior, such as

[57] Coquery-Vidrovitch, *The History of African Cities*, 135–169. [58] Ibid., 169–173.

Benin City, Kumasi, and Abomey, used their resources and their lineage- or spiritual-based political power to extend protections against enslavement to, and command subjugation from, their neighbors. Their involvement in slave trading, and the wealth it generated, helped to preserve their autonomy and expand their regional authority. Meanwhile, urban slave trading communities on the Atlantic coast, such as Anomabo, Lagos, and Ouidah grew in prominence over time. Their involvement in the slave trade built up local merchant elites who used their newfound wealth and influence to challenge the rulership of older elites.[59] In both cases, unfolding changes to urban political and material cultures and economic practices were largely informed by indigenous ambitions. These towns and cities mediated Atlantic encounters to serve African interests. But they also marked the geographic reach of African power in Atlantic affairs. After departing African cities and ports, goods and more importantly enslaved people were aggressively commodified and became the source of capital that benefited primarily Europeans.[60]

The West Central African port cities of Luanda and Benguela, founded in 1576 and 1617 respectively, exemplify cases where Europeans successfully used towns to consolidate colonial claims in Africa. Both sites were founded by the Portuguese to serve as the capital city of a colony. They were built to house imperial and urban institutions, such as the governor's residence, the municipal council, and Catholic churches. Additionally, through their ports, merchants, and artisans, Luanda and Benguela became important nodes within the urban network that serviced European ships en route to other parts of the Atlantic and to the Indian Ocean. The two cities also supported Portugal's direct trading relationships and political alliances with various peoples in the West Central African hinterland, enabling what most other Europeans failed to achieve elsewhere in Africa. But even in these two cities, conceived as urban extensions of Portugal's imperial power, everyday activities were shaped by indigenous practices and interests, from the operation of markets to the workings of households to the politics of urban–rural exchanges.[61] In time, these and other coastal cities would facilitate full-blown European imperialism in Africa, but in the first two centuries of the early modern era their role in that process was tentative at best.

In the Americas, Europeans wielded urbanization as a tool of imperial expansion more consistently and more effectively, as Spanish efforts at the

[59] Ibid., 183–195; Mann, *Slavery and the Birth of an African City*, 23–31; Law, *Ouidah*, 20–45; Shumway, *The Fante*, 71–75; Sparks, *The Two Princes*, 33–69.

[60] Smallwood, *Saltwater Slavery*, 33–64; Johnson, *Wicked Flesh*, 16–50.

[61] Santos, "Luanda: A Colonial City"; Candido, *An African Slaving Port*, 31–88; Heywood, *Njinga of Angola*, 18–34.

turn of the fifteenth to the sixteenth century illustrate. During his second voyage to the Caribbean, after finding fort La Navidad destroyed and its residents dead, Christopher Columbus ordered the construction of the town of Isabela. With its tower, storehouse, church, and the captain general's (i.e. Columbus's) residence built in stone, Isabela was meant to serve as a hub of colonial activities while supporting a more permanent and imposing Spanish presence in Hispaniola. Assailed by hurricanes, subjected to Columbus's despotic tendencies, and distant from gold mines and Indigenous communities the Spanish could trade with and demand labor from, this town too was unable to survive. The idea that urbanization was essential to imperial expansion did not, however, suffer in the process. The first royal governor appointed to Hispaniola was instructed by Queen Isabella to establish towns to avoid the dispersal of settlers.[62] The island's capital was then moved to the island's southern coast, where a new town, Santo Domingo, was built.[63]

The pairing of town creation and imperial pursuits also featured prominently in Hernán Cortés's campaign in Mesoamerica. In 1519, following unsuccessful campaigns to establish a Spanish presence on the mainland, Cortés led a military expedition of more than 400 men through the Yucatán. Cortés, then a subaltern of the governor of Cuba, had limited authority and ability to take legal action against or in alliance with the Indigenous peoples he encountered. To circumvent the problem, he hurriedly established the town of Villa Rica de la Vera Cruz, justifying in this manner the election of a governing council and his own election as alcalde and chief justice. Able to claim the legal authority to enforce Spanish interests, Cortés set off to demand the vassalage of the powerful Aztec city of Tenochtitlán.[64]

The fate of Tenochtitlán after a brutal siege and military defeat illustrates further the urban strategies of early modern Spanish imperialism. The vibrant capital of the Mexica people, whose influence extended far into its hinterland, had been an important political and economic center in Mesoamerica. After the destruction of much of its governing elite and part of its cityscape, Cortés and his followers put the city's past centrality to work for their own goals. Rebuilt into Mexico City, the city continued to facilitate trade, religious and political pageantry, and the distribution of material and intangible resources. Even as the city continued to invoke its recent Indigenous past, those seeking what it had to offer increasingly did so under Spanish terms and in spaces that projected Spain's intended political, economic, and cultural supremacy.[65]

62 Kagan, *Urban Images*, 28; Altman, *Life and Society*, 20–26.
63 Deagan and Cruxent, *Columbus's Outpost*; Altman, "Key to the Indies."
64 Kagan, *Urban Images*, 28–29; Townsend, *Malintzin's Choices*, 43–44.
65 Candiani, *Dreaming of Dry Land*, 1–14; Mundy, *The Death of Aztec Tenochtitlan*, 1–24, 72–98.

Indigenous cities throughout Mesoamerica endured similar trajectories to that of Tenochtitlán. Their public buildings were replaced by the *cabildo* (which housed the municipal council and local court), the residences of Spanish elites, and Catholic churches and monasteries. As much as possible, these constructions, the symbols of Spanish authority, were organized around a main square from where straight streets reached out in a gridiron or checkered pattern to the city's urban and then rural periphery. Activities in these thoroughfares and squares, moreover, were set to the rhythm of Spanish colonial everyday and ceremonial life. By conquering and transforming the urban realities of Indigenous Americans, imperial Spain aimed to organize the production of colonial wealth, govern its colonial subjects, and control the labor of native peoples.[66]

The process of hispanicization of urban life in the Americas was often upset, however, by the strength of Indigenous urban traditions. The Spanish may have founded some towns and cities or taken over Indigenous ones in Meso- and South America, but as Abraham Ortelius's maps of Peru and the Tamaulipas Coast of Mexico illustrate, the native urban imprint in these regions was inescapable (Figure 4). The early history of the cities of Cuzco and Lima is a case in point. Located, respectively, in the Andean highlands and on the Pacific coast of modern-day Peru, these cities were not Atlantic per se. Their trajectories were nevertheless tightly connected to processes unfolding around the Spanish Atlantic world. In Cuzco, like in Tenochtitlán, a war of conquest was followed by efforts to take the city and its buildings for the Spanish crown and its subjects. Inca elites, however, successfully mobilized an army that temporarily reasserted control over the city and posed a serious threat to Spanish encroachment. Despite their defeat, Cuzco remained a strong enclave of Inca cultural and political memory. It was Lima therefore, the coastal city founded by Francisco Pizarro to assert his supremacy over his enemies and allies, that became the seat of the viceroyalty. Lima's newly minted urban layout, cityscape, and political and religious pageantry were meant to cement Spanish imperial claims in Peru.[67]

Spain's urban colonial project also involved efforts to resettle Indigenous populations in European-styled towns to be civilized, converted, and ultimately integrated into the Spanish empire as useful subjects.[68] But here, too, Spanish imperial plans were regularly upset by existing Indigenous urban realities. The most dramatic example of this urban project, and of its shortcomings, was Viceroy of Peru Francisco de Toledo's attempt to relocate Indigenous

[66] Kagan, *Urban Images*, 30–33; Clendinnen, *Ambivalent Conquests*, 39–41.
[67] Osorio, *Inventing Lima*, 35–56.
[68] Martinez, "Group Identities in Puebla de los Angeles," 14–15.

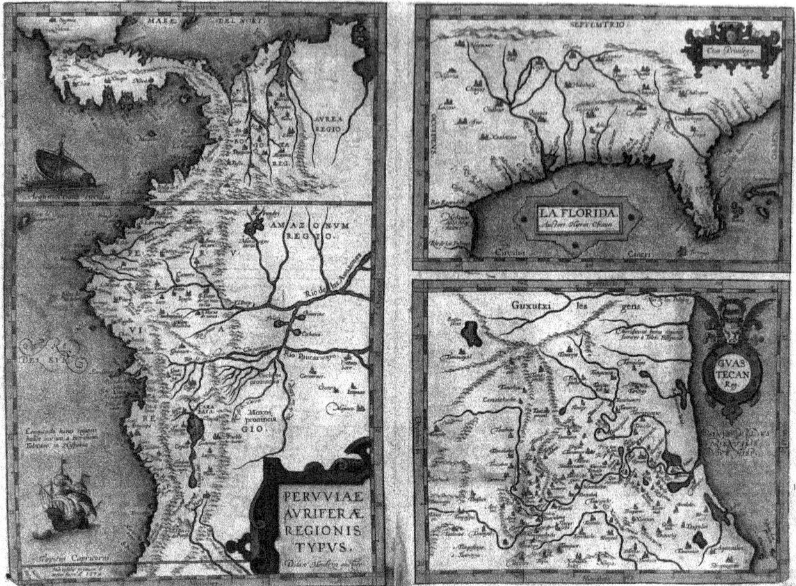

Figure 4 Cities, towns, and villages in the auriferous region of Peru and the Huasteca region (1584).

Abraham Ortelius, *Pervviae avriferae regionis typvs / La Florida / auctore Hieron. Chiaues; Gvastecan reg.* (Antwerp: Christophe Plantin, ?, 1584) Map. www.loc.gov/item/84696980/.

communities to newly built towns, or *reducciones*. The resettlement aimed to counter political and economic threats posed by powerful Indigenous leaders (*caciques*), the demographic collapse of Native populations, and settler conflicts over access to land and labor. With their straight streets, individual family houses, a main square with a church, an Indigenous cabildo, and a jail, the new towns would discourage illicit or idolatrous behaviors and support a local government that could undermine the *caciques*. The concentration of Andeans in fewer *reducciones*, moreover, would facilitate the collection of taxes and labor tribute.[69]

The very scope and difficulty of Toledo's resettlement project prevented it from ever being fully realized. Towns were only partially built, and their unfavorable location and lack of resources failed to attract or retain their intended residents. People made every effort, moreover, to return to their original lands and communities, moving as much as possible between their assigned towns and the places to which they felt connected. Relating to towns as administrative or religious

69 Mumford, *Vertical Empire*, 85–98; Herzog, "Indigenous *Reducciones*," 9–30.

centers, and not year-round places of residence, had after all been the norm under the Inca. In time, this urban project succeeded nonetheless in disrupting Andean communities and land uses and displacing hundreds of thousands of people. Spanish authorities enabled land grabbing by settlers when they designated the land of resettled Andeans as empty. Forced compliance with labor tribute demands also caused relocations that further destabilized local economies and increased Andean dependency on the resources of emerging towns.[70] The urban reorganization of colonial Peru may not have realized the urban ideals of imperial agents; it nevertheless advanced colonial goals.

Spain was not unique in its use of towns and cities to cement empire in the Americas. Directives to establish urban centers, with the understanding that they were crucial to the pursuit of imperial political, economic, and ideological goals, are evident in other colonial settings. The Portuguese crown, for example, while using the system of donatary captaincies to promote the colonization of the Atlantic islands and later of South America, included the provision that captain generals found one or more towns on their concession. Captaincies in Brazil were large tracts of land mostly left unsettled by the Portuguese. Their capital cities, however, formed a distinct urban geography where Portuguese political and religious power was on display and enforced.[71]

The Portuguese colonial project in the Americas also included the urban resettlement of Indigenous peoples to reorganize their everyday living, labor, and economic activities. Native communities in Brazil were encouraged or forced to relocate to *aldeias* (villages), many organized as religious missions and overseen by the Jesuit Order. These places, with their huts, gardens, streets, squares, and chapels, were meant to offer more than Catholic instruction. They aimed to transform traditional native domestic and community life, as well as labor and production practices, into something more akin to European ones. Indigenous people, forced to contend with hostile Portuguese settlers and the threat of enslavement, turned some *aldeias* into physical and legal safe havens. In the built structures of their newfound communities, they gathered the resources to shield themselves from attacks. Deploying the legal standing of the *aldeia* in petitions to the crown, moreover, they mobilized royal protections.[72]

Latecomers to empire building in the Americas similarly relied on towns and cities to claim territory and resources. When the Dutch took over the captaincy of Pernambuco from the Portuguese in the late sixteenth century, they built up

70 Mumford, *Vertical Empire*, 119–156.

71 Newitt, *A History of Portuguese Overseas Expansion*, 127–129; Vidal, "Une Fondation Atlantique."

72 Metcalf, "The Society of Jesus and the First *Aldeias*"; Chrysostomo, "L'urbanisation des marges de la colonie."

the once small secondary town of Recife to serve as the capital of their colony. From there, Dutch imperial agents sought control over the region's sugar plantation economy and the trade in enslaved Africans in Elmina and Luanda. After their defeat by Portuguese imperial and colonial forces who reclaimed the captaincy for Portugal, the Dutch took their colonial ambitions to the Caribbean and North America. Their new-gained experience with sugar production and slave trading in Pernambuco informed their subsequent efforts. The urban strategies they had put in place in Recife helped, as well, to adjust their own strong urban traditions and policies to colonial realities.[73]

English settlers, companies, and investors in North America also viewed urban development as important to organizing space, people, resources, and trade. The Puritan towns of early seventeenth-century Massachusetts and and the town of Savannah, Georgia, for example, were the product of a utopian effort to create a better society than the one left behind. In the plantation colonies of Maryland and Virginia, political elites legislated the creation of towns to preserve the loyalty of English subjects who might be led astray by Native polities, other European empires, or newfound economic possibilities. Towns, they hoped, would prevent population dispersal, loss of colonial profits, and political degeneration.[74] By the turn of the seventeenth to the eighteenth century, few of these urban efforts rivaled the main Spanish colonial capitals. Some never existed beyond paper or the imaginings of their planners. They, nevertheless, reflected a colonial project intent on establishing urban nodes that could join politically, economically, and ideologically disparate parts of the English empire.

The praying towns of the Massachusetts Bay colony illustrate, moreover, Puritan settlers' own urban project of religious and cultural conversion of the Indigenous population. The missionary John Eliot was instrumental in the establishment of fourteen settlements that, by the start of King Philip's war in 1675, concentrated around 2,000 people. He and his fellow Puritan leaders calculated that Indigenous people would be more inclined to accept Christianity and service to the colony if they lived in English-styled urban communities. Archaeological evidence reveals, however, that in the case of Natick, founded in 1651, the town was organized more like other Indigenous villages than in the manner envisioned by Eliot.[75] Native peoples in what became Massachusetts had well-established traditions of village life on which they relied to cultivate

[73] Middleton, "'How It Came That Bakers Bake No Bread'"; Hurk, "Plan versus Execution"; Klooster, *The Dutch Moment*, 33–73.

[74] Reps, *Tidewater Towns*; Lounsbury, *The Courthouses of Early Virginia*, 49–54; Musselwhite, *Urban Dreams*, 4–12.

[75] Rubin, *Tears of Repentance*, 19–38; Stanley, "Praying Indian Towns."

ties of obligation and affection between them. When relocated to praying towns, they drew from their own urban experiences to survive the disruption caused by European presence.

European urban experiments in the Americas may have pursued Native subjugation to European ideals of morality, civility, and domesticity. They may have even advanced the hegemonic power of European political, economic, and religious institutions. But here, like on the African Atlantic coast, they could not fully escape the influence of Indigenous urban experiences. Native populations in the Western Hemisphere, similar to those in West and Central Africa, had relied on urban communities to defend their resources and their political interests for centuries. They would continue to do so as they navigated the impact of the nearby European presence. West African villages in the Gold Coast, which grew in the vicinity of European forts, are one example of the connection between urbanization and the pursuit of new opportunities for trade and local dominance. The Creek town of Okfuskee, founded in the early eighteenth century inland from the colonies of South Carolina and Georgia, is another.[76] Yet even where Indigenous peoples lost the autonomy to establish and govern their own cities and towns, they found ways to imprint their own priorities onto urban places.

Conclusion

Between the fifteenth and seventeenth centuries, people, goods, and ideas increasingly moved across the Atlantic Ocean. These populations and their products often originated, arrived, and met in the villages, towns, and cities of Europe, Africa, and the Americas. The primacy of urban places in the history of early Atlantic economic and political encounters was not accidental. Cities, towns, and villages in all three continents had articulated local and regional trade, cultural exchange, and political and economic power for decades, if not centuries. They would continue to support commercial networks, the dissemination of shared habits, and the enforcement of elite interests, but increasingly over larger and more complex geographies. Moreover, urban lessons learned across a century or two prior to Atlantic encounters helped to dictate urban strategies subsequently. Such was particularly true of Europeans, whose experiences with fortifications, trading outposts, and municipal governance informed their efforts to carve out spatial enclaves in Africa and the Americas. In time, Europeans' idealizations of the city clouded their perception of the morality, sophistication, and even sovereignty of African and American societies. As they assessed the foreignness and

[76] Piker, *Okfuskee*, 15–44.

the strength of Indigenous African and American cities, Europeans adjusted the policies they adopted toward the peoples they encountered.

Neither the urban nor the imperial designs of Europeans in Africa and the Americas were predestined to succeed, to be sure. Yet the conviction that certain urban forms and institutions could reorient Indigenous politics and economy toward their interests ensured a stubborn persistence of European urban projects and, through them, affirmation of European prerogatives. As this section has shown, the establishment of urban enclaves, whether forts and factories, occupied Indigenous towns and cities, or newly founded ones, characterized early European expansionist efforts around the Atlantic. These settlements did not always produce the commanding urban societies European rulers, merchants, and colonists idealized. In Africa, they were more likely to become dependent on neighboring and allied Indigenous cities and towns. In the Americas, Indigenous populations continued to use urban places for community support and economic survival according to their own long-standing practices. Still, the intercontinental urban networks that emerged from these early Atlantic encounters, and that Europeans tried to control, ultimately directed wealth and resources toward rising European imperial centers.

3 Cities and Atlantic Empires

In 1741, during the War of Jenkins's Ear between the empires of Great Britain and Spain, the London publisher Henry Overton produced and commercialized a map of the West Indies (Figure 5). Maps had become by then a relatively common consumer good, demanded by a British public interested in visualizing Britain's global prominence and involvement in overseas conflicts.[77] This map aimed to inform its users about the West Indies, where so much imperial trade took place. As a further appeal to those curious about that part of the world, it was "adorn'd with prospects of ye most considerable towns, ports, harbours &tc. therein contained from the latest & best observations." Noticeable in the depiction of these mostly Spanish colonial cities and towns – Boston and New York being the exception – is the representation of forts and waterfronts replete with trading vessels. The two towns on the bottom left and right of the map, Porto Bello and Chagre, respectively, also illustrate British naval attacks against the Spanish. The inclusion of these urban images is telling. Even as they call attention to the differences in size and complexity between Cartagena and Panama City, or Mexico City and Vera Cruz, they reveal contemporary views of urban places as critical hubs in the articulation of an

[77] Pedley and Edney, *The History of Cartography*, 510.

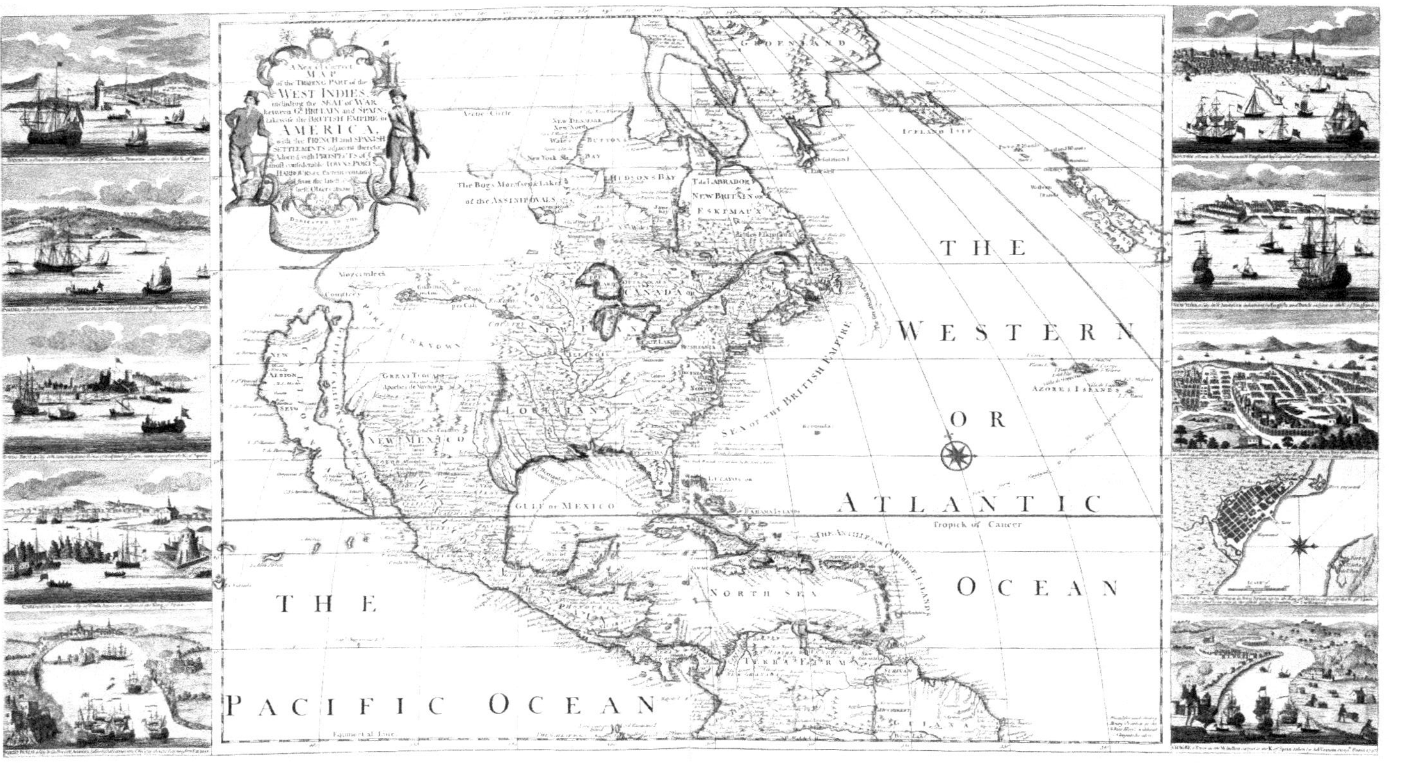

Figure 5 "Map of the trading part of the West Indies . . . with . . . the most considerable towns, ports, harbours" (1741).

Lionel Pincus and Princess Firyal Map Division, The New York Public Library. "A new & correct map of the trading part of the West Indies," New York Public Library Digital Collections. https://digitalcollections.nypl.org/items/510d47da-ef42-a3d9-e040-e00a18064a99.

eighteenth-century Atlantic world. These towns and cities, the map communicates, had vital importance to commercial exchange and the defense of empire.

Indeed, Atlantic towns and cities were key to the progressive consolidation of a European imperial presence within the Atlantic basin. Between the late 1600s and 1800, from La Rochelle to New Orleans, Bristol to Philadelphia, Ouidah to Salvador, Seville to Cartagena, cities articulated transoceanic networks of exchange. It was a process that relied on existing cities, while also prompting the foundation of new ones. As the number of cities increased, so did their influence over the built environment, population, and political workings of the Atlantic world. Numerous flourishing towns thus rose in prominence to become the anchors of the Western imperial project. Others, though sustained by the political leadership and economic entrepreneurship of non-Europeans, helped to feed European capital accumulation and commercial power.

Atlantic cities were hubs of connectivity. They were also islands in a vast oceanic system that was, compared to our contemporary global world, thinly networked. Their physical distance from one another created obstacles to the imperial pursuit of political, economic, and cultural congruity over geographical expanses. This reality, in turn, threatened the success and profitability of the colonial and trade enterprises imagined by European monarchs, elites, and merchants. As European settlers and their white descendants ventured throughout the Atlantic, however, they often countered the challenge of distance with the establishment of familiar urban institutions and practices. Political offices, courts of law, pillories and gallows, wharves and custom houses, mints, markets, and even public parades and processions imbued urban places with recognizable urban activities in ways that minimized the abstraction of empire. In this manner, cities both coastal and inland did more than facilitate exchanges. They mediated and materialized imperial transatlantic connections and enabled tangible shared experiences, generating continuity for those living and transiting within the Atlantic world.

Careful analysis of urban sites and places that manifested political, legal, religious, and economic power uncovers how European empires and their white subjects used urban infrastructure to fulfill their ambitions. It also reveals the false starts and missteps of European imperial projects that were repeatedly challenged by African and Native American populations who aimed to shape urban life in the service of their own interests. Importantly, though, these groups' interactions with each other under the aegis of various Atlantic urban institutions helped to cement the ties between these places and European metropolitan and white prerogatives. Atlantic cities thus contributed to the increasingly asymmetrical distribution of power within the early modern world.

Sites of Power

By the 1400s, most colonizing powers in the Atlantic knew cities as effective vehicles of political power. Through construction and the concentration of ruling officials, cities were used by the invaders to legitimize their imperial incursions to multiple audiences. Yet, as much as they served as technologies of European rulership, local, regional, and Atlantic contingencies imposed limits on their power. The non-European inhabitants of this world often resisted European encroachment that could not be manipulated for their benefit. As a technology of rulership, therefore, the European-built city continued to confront challenges to the realization of its purpose. Its very real limitations were nowhere more obvious than in West Africa, where Europeans still failed to claim much territory in the early nineteenth century.

Newly founded and newly occupied cities were designed to anchor the foundations of early modern European power. In the course of their development, some achieved this through the expansion of two powerful institutions: the church and the royal state. As a means of enforcing this power, legal institutions buttressed secular and godly authority. Their importance was exemplified by the pride of place their physical expressions were given in the growing urban landscape. Although Dutch, French, Spanish, Portuguese, and British city plans were not identical, all placed the church, the residence of the political leadership, and the seat of the law at the heart of the town.

Whether in a transatlantic or regional town, a visitor would find these institutions housed in the city's most splendid buildings situated in prominent locations on the water or on the main squares and thoroughfares. In Paris, the Louvre and Notre Dame were the epicenter of the city, while London had Whitehall and St Paul's Cathedral. Meanwhile, Cap Français incorporated a governor's house and multiple Catholic churches just as Charleston featured a state house and two Anglican churches.

In the Spanish Americas, expressions of urban power were fully enmeshed with the design of the conquest. Catholic monastic orders, the church, and secular governance, united by legal authority, were all sited at the center of the *traza* – the uniform grid plan that located imperial power in its central square. Power was embodied in the buildings that bordered the plaza mayor – the Catholic Church, the governor's residence, the cabildo, and the cloisters. In these grand edifices, the ceremonies and formalities of colonial governance were elaborated by an ever-growing cadre of royal agents, making political decisions in the name of the king. In the centuries following the conquest, the legal and financial basis of this power only increased as churches and religious orders accumulated property, as bureaucracy multiplied, and as bodies of law came into conversation with one another in the colonial urban setting.[78]

Mexico City and Lima, the capitals of the two viceroyalties of New Spain and Peru, were the chief locations in which the Law of Castile met the Law of the Indies. Whether on the site of a former Indigenous empire, as Mexico City was, or in a new place founded by colonists to assert their authority, like Lima, authority converged on the central square. Regular promotion of public festivities to celebrate a royal birth or marriage, the arrival of a new viceroy, or a religious date further transformed urban spaces into places of imperial power. These events turned squares, streets, and the balconies of government buildings into stages where that power could be performed with pomp and circumstance. The participation of Indigenous and African parties in these public ceremonies, often cast in a subordinate role and made to enact their embrace of the Spanish monarch and the Catholic Church, helped to create an urban visual language of racial hierarchy and Spanish supremacy.[79]

This power flowed beyond the viceregal capital through its re-instantiation in the provincial town. These smaller towns lacked the Audencia (High Court) and Inquisition of the capitals, but they still enjoyed an intricate colonial bureaucracy that had the *alcaldes mayores* at its center. The office – part judge and part mayor – was put up for sale by the crown after 1675, leading to a renewed intensification of imperial infrastructure building. Assisted by many other petty officials, called *oficiales subalternos* or *ministros inferiores*, these Spanish-born men ensured that justice and order were the centerpieces of the townscape. Sporadic visitations from metropolitan officials ensured that they were adhering to core imperial values, just as Inquisition and episcopal visits enforced conformity to Catholic beliefs.

The urban qualities of Mesoamerican and Andean Indigenous societies, and the propensity of colonists to cluster in towns, made it especially easy for Spain to consolidate political and religious power in the urban environment. Nevertheless, most Dutch, French, English, and Portuguese towns featured similar physical expressions of colonial political power in their cityscapes. In New York, the role of the city as an imperial hub came into view during the transition from the possession of one empire to another in 1664, when the English seized the colony of New Netherland from the Dutch.

A republic of city-states, the Dutch had excelled at using towns as weapons of imperial expansion across their Asian and Atlantic territories. When they arrived in the Hudson River Valley in 1609, they immediately established two

[78] Burkholder and Johnson, *Colonial Latin America*.

[79] Dean, *Inka Bodies*, 7–22; Curcio-Nagy, *Great Festivals*, 1–14; Osorio, *Inventing Lima*, 61–70.

towns: Albany, which was upriver and designed as a fur-trading post, and New Amsterdam, a port on the island of Manhattan, in the territory of the Lenape people. At the moment of conquest by the English fifty-five years later, New Amsterdam had a fully functioning city council, a number of guilds, and a Dutch Reformed church. These institutions underpinned a strong civic culture and a clear model of the good citizen: a man who advanced the colony's development through his adherence to the laws that regulated trade and preserved the common good. On a 1661 map of the town, the church and the governor's house are prominently depicted as symbols of colonial authority in this urban outpost (Figure 6).[80]

With the English conquest came the need to imprint an Anglo version of urban order on the newly named New York. The process of replacing Dutch

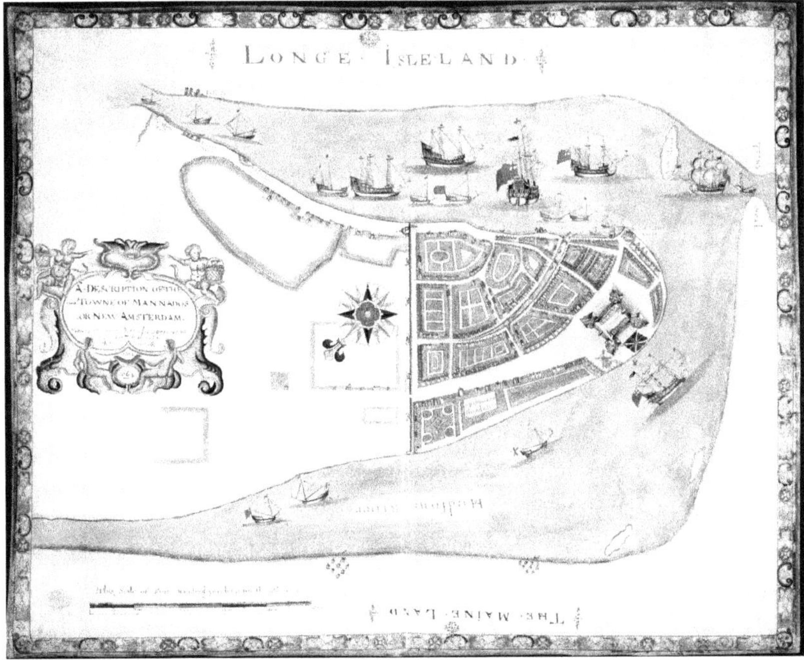

Figure 6 "A Description of the Towne of Mannados or New Amsterdam . . . 1661."

Norman B. Leventhal Map & Education Center, "A DESCRIPTION OF THE TOWNE OF MANNADOS OR NEW AMSTERDAM as it was in September 1661 lying in Latitude 40 de: and 40,: Anno Domini 1664." https://collections.leventhalmap.org/search/commonwealth:hx11z598v.

[80] Herk, "Plan versus Execution."

civic institutions with English ones was slow and plagued by conflict. English government was more hierarchical and less attentive to the voices of all its citizens, especially non-elites. The English governor Nicolls consolidated his power both within New York itself and over surrounding Long Island settlements. Poorer free white city people felt excluded from government and deprived of the political and economic privileges they had enjoyed under Dutch rule. Political tumult in England with the rise of James II's autocratic and Catholic monarchy, followed by its fall at the Glorious Revolution in 1688, brought factionalism and rebellion to the city. Once all was said and done and the age of British imperial ascendancy dawned after 1700, however, New York remained the center of power and the seat of imperial governance in the colony. If anything, the grip of wealthy Europeans on power intensified as Anglo-Dutch families consolidated urban and rural landholdings to become an unassailable elite in all parts of the colony. By the middle of the eighteenth century, New York was home to almost 12,000 people, making it a sizable city replete with the spaces and buildings that projected the strength of British imperial and civic power.[81]

The English were just as eager to leverage the urban assets of the Spanish after their invasion of Jamaica in 1655. Targeting the island's capital, St Iago de la Vega, Cromwell's forces succeeded in establishing their supremacy by 1658. The invaders then set about securing their claim by building the commercial center of Port Royal and renaming the place they had inherited Spanish Town. With the island a hub of piracy and privateering, the port grew rapidly until an earthquake sent it tumbling into the sea in 1696. This did not deter the English, who started a new commercial center in Kingston. Because of the preeminence of the Spanish administrative capital, Jamaica persisted in having two urban hubs – one political and one commercial – all the way until 1872, when the functions were consolidated in Kingston following the end of direct British rule. The English saw the advantage of already-established government buildings, supplementing them with Anglican churches and public squares that would enhance Spanish Town's "ancient glory."[82]

In both New York and Jamaica, a substantial number of urban inhabitants were free and enslaved Africans, deemed inferior by ruling Europeans. These rulers used public urban spaces to brutalize and shame any such people who challenged their domination. Almost every Atlantic city in the Americas made squares, or the areas around major public buildings, into theaters of punishment. There, Europeans performed brute expressions of colonial power by exploiting

[81] Middleton, *From Privileges to Rights*, 53–95.

[82] Robertson, *Gone Is the Ancient Glory*; Pestana, *English Conquest of Jamaica*.

the force of their legal codes. Mexico City publicly hosted *autos-da-fé*, Inquisition-led rituals of condemnation and punishment for religious heresy. Bridgetown, in British Barbados, had its "cage" where freedom-seeking enslaved people were imprisoned in view of passersby. More customary were the stocks and whipping posts imported from the European town and sited in the marketplaces of towns such as Charleston, South Carolina.[83]

White criminals and "disobedient" enslaved Africans who challenged elite European supremacy received a public chastising in these urban spaces while the crowds looked on. Sometimes, the spectacle was a hanging and sometimes it included the process of being "whipped through" the streets to maximize the shaming potential of the punishment. When subaltern people were suspected of revolt – such as in the New York Conspiracy of 1741 – the mass hangings and burnings at the stake that resulted took place in the city. Although Tacky's Revolt in Jamaica was principally a rural affair, Spanish Town, the island's capital, and Kingston, its commercial hub, were marshaled as instruments of repression. While the Assembly passed new laws to try and restrict the mobility of enslaved people, condemned rebels were collected in Kingston and either hanged or deported on ships bound for other British colonial locations.[84] As a conglomeration of people and institutions, the urban form alone had the qualities and infrastructure necessary to make such events into displays of power visible to diverse crowds of people.

Yet these very same qualities of density and populousness were what made growing urban spaces full of opportunity for the peoples of these Atlantic societies. Cities rapidly became a destination for Africans seeking freedom from enslavement. Some individuals resorted to towns because of economic opportunity, while others fled to them so that they might get lost in the crowd. Often, these freedom seekers could find accommodation in the quarters of free Black city dwellers. It was also easier to blend into the crowded public spaces of the city. In transatlantic hubs, demand for sailors was constant, making escape as a crewmember on a ship an alluring possibility.[85]

Although cities could be a refuge for enslaved people, they were also an environment in which subalterns lived in the shadow of the levers of imperial power. In the British Atlantic city, Black communities were usually forced to exist on the margins of imperial political and religious institutions. Even so, marginalized people used the density of the city to organize themselves. These efforts eventually resulted in the establishment of Black churches and friendly societies, such as Philadelphia's African Methodist Episcopal (AME)

[83] Curcio-Nagy, *Great Festivals,* 31–32; Fuentes, *Dispossessed Lives*, 13–45.
[84] Zabin, *Dangerous Economies*, 132–158; Brown, *Tacky's Revolt*, 208–236.
[85] Equiano, *Interesting Narrative*; Burnard and Hart, "Kingston and Charleston."

congregation and Charleston's Brown Fellowship Society.[86] Taking advantage of their incorporated status, some Black-led organizations purchased urban real estate and built houses of worship.

These converts to Protestantism may have encountered European proselytizers who supported their initial conversion to Christianity. The English evangelical network led by Lady Selina Huntington embraced Black Christians, including the Boston poet Phillis Wheatley and the Charleston free Black resident John Marrant. Such individuals received a frosty reception from Protestant authorities who did not support the conversion of the enslaved.[87] In the Iberian city, Indigenous non-elites had greater success in appropriating urban religious institutions and reimagining them to better suit the advancement of their communities and interests. This was in part because the Catholic Church allowed Indigenous people from Africa, Asia, and America some access to religious fraternal life, extending them limited legal and property-owning privileges.[88]

As Catholics, Indigenous and African peoples in Central and South American cities pursued strategies that allowed them to build useful alliances across families and institutions in the districts of the city where they lived, beyond the elite imperial core. In the New Spanish regional hub of Puebla de los Angeles, founded in 1531, its enslaved African residents had all obtained their freedom by the early eighteenth century. They had realized their own manumission by fulfilling essential roles in urban institutions, such as Puebla's convents. Their work won them income and patrons, who eventually opened up a route to freedom. Indigenous people in Mexico City similarly used imperial institutions for their own purposes when they established their own parallel church infrastructures in the *barrio*. Called the "false church" by the Spanish Catholic hierarchy, who nevertheless tolerated it, it thrived as an institution that combined Christian and Indigenous beliefs to produce a hybrid religion that was the bedrock of the community.[89]

Across the seventeenth and eighteenth centuries, the Atlantic city, as it evolved in the Americas, became an engine of imperial power even while it developed into a place of opportunity for Indigenous and African peoples. Importantly, however, this was not yet a universal state of affairs in an Atlantic world under construction. While Europeans were establishing urban authority in the Americas, they were in no position to increase their influence in Africa. Jessica Marie Johnson has described how, at this time, Saint Louis-

[86] Nash, *Forging Freedom*, 130–134; Johnson and Roark, *Black Masters*, 212–216.
[87] Tyson, "Lady Huntingdon, Religion, and Race."
[88] Hidalgo and Valerio, "Negotiating Status through Confraternal practices."
[89] Sierra Silva, *Urban Slavery*, 76–106; O'Hara, "Orthodox Underworld."

and Gorée in Senegambia were not a symbols of European colonization but rather a places where the French "entered a complex web of social and commercial relations created by Africans themselves."[90] There was a similar balance of power in most of the other West African conurbations in existence at this time. Both places that were founded as European forts, such as Elmina, and towns with African origins, like Ouidah, were controlled by people indigenous to the continent. With political power residing firmly in the interior of kingdoms such as Songhai and Kongo, whose leaders identified European-inhabited port towns as commercial entrepôts operating for their benefit, there was scant opportunity for the establishment of imperial institutions of political, religious, and legal power.[91]

An exception to this arrangement, emerging in Angola in the second half of the eighteenth century, was the Portuguese-founded towns of Luanda and Benguela. Since African power in this region was centered far from the coast, Europeans were able to populate these small towns with institutions of government and law without challenge. In 1779, Benguela welcomed its first town governor – a development that heralded a drive to tighten imperial control by elaborating a colonial administration that had previously been much less comprehensive than its American counterpart. Although the town remained small, with just a few thousand inhabitants, Europeans' efforts to impose themselves included the construction of new public buildings.[92]

Indeed, the history of imperial power in Portuguese Angola's towns is instructive precisely because of these very visible limitations. Even in Atlantic cities where European colonists seemed to achieve urban hegemony, barriers nevertheless emerged quickly to challenge the unbridled exercise of authority. Such barriers mirrored those encountered in Luanda and Benguela. It thus remained impossible to achieve influence beyond cities whose rural and oceanic hinterlands were so vast, especially when these hinterlands were populated with indigenous people with their own long-established religious and political systems.

The outcome of these challenges was a situation, by the middle of the eighteenth century, in which some cities had sowed the seeds of imperial mastery. Nevertheless, the Atlantic city had failed to completely fulfill European imperial ambitions of creating cultural or even political hegemony. The governor's house, the church, and the law courts became symbols of colonial authority that stood tall in many an Atlantic urban cityscape. However, their presence did not represent the total conquest of the Atlantic world by Europeans. Through using, inhabiting, and owning urban space, Indigenous and African peoples put it to work for their

---

[90] Johnson, *Wicked Flesh*, 16–50. [91] Saupin, "Emergence of Port Towns"; Law, *Ouidah*.

[92] Ferreira, *Cross-Cultural Exchange*, 20–51.

own ends. In the majority of West Africa, Africans remained so powerful that Europeans were unable to establish any meaningful political or religious authority in the coastal towns where they resided. Although in the Americas Black and Indigenous investment in the European institutions of political and religious power had the effect of legitimizing them, it also ensured that they did not enjoy uncontested supremacy.

Sites of Trade

A system of trade and circulation set in motion by growing towns was essential to the articulation of the Atlantic's early modern empires. As they facilitated economic exchange, cities grew and changed in ways that reflected the characteristics of this emerging oceanic entity. Most particularly, they were places that could house the ports, wharves, warehouses, and counting houses necessary for high-volume, long-distance trade to develop. Such spaces could not evolve without a host of supporting infrastructures that cities also had in abundance. As centers of skilled labor, of services, and of marketplaces for food, drink, and manufactured goods, towns supplied the necessities that supported the dramatic expansion of oceanic trade that made this Atlantic world. Across transatlantic, regional, and local hubs, this was an intimate and critical relationship.

As dense and elaborate economic systems, cities acted as launch pads for trade. Yet, of course, it was the urban population who set commerce in motion and financed its growth. In London, city merchants plowed resources into trade in new, Atlantic locales. Men like Gilbert Heathcote, a trader with modest, provincial origins, seized the economic opportunities of empire to become rich and influential. Heathcote made his fortune through commerce and army contracts in Jamaica, dying in 1733 as a member of parliament and former Mayor of London.[93] Although Bristol had long been a mercantile city, Liverpool and Glasgow grew from insignificant towns to commercial powerhouses as their residents tapped into the opportunity of dealing in people, sugar, tobacco, and other colonial commodities. Along with London, these provincial cities forged connections with equally dynamic towns in Britain's North American and Caribbean colonies. Boston, New York, Newport, Philadelphia, Charleston, and Kingston all hosted trading communities that were connected by people, credit, and shipping routes in an ever-denser network of exchange.[94]

The centrality of these ports was assisted by widespread early modern beliefs concerning commerce. In the eyes of most early modern imperialists, trade was a zero-sum game in which the winners were the empires who succeeded best at

[93] Zahedieh, *Capital and the Colonies*, 131–136.
[94] Hancock, *Citizens of the World*; Morgan, *Bristol and the Atlantic Trade*.

reserving for themselves the economic bounty of colonization. While complete autarky was rarely the ultimate goal, being too reliant on another country for manufactured goods or raw materials was considered to be a source of national weakness. In the context of this mercantilist philosophy, port cities were first and foremost places where protected communities of merchants could control economic exchange by keeping the traders of foreign nations out of an empire's commercial networks.[95]

Spain's imperial cities especially excelled at this practice. Towns on both sides of the Atlantic housed an elaborate regulatory infrastructure that was embedded within the urban landscape. The Casa de Contratación de las Indias, established at Seville in 1503 and relocated to Cadiz in 1717, oversaw all aspects of Spanish Atlantic trade, from the licensing of merchants to the regulation of harbor infrastructure. The Casa's tight grip on commerce made it difficult for foreign merchants to get a share of Spain's lucrative trade, except when the government explicitly chose to sell access, as it did with the slave trade's *asiento*. These metropolitan institutions were supported by an Atlantic-wide system of regulation. Periodic urban fairs, like those at Portobello and Cartagena (depicted in Figure 5), hosted the exchange of European goods for colonial products such as gold, silver, gems, coffee, sugar, and cocoa. In recognition of the high value of the precious metals, American wares were transported back to Europe by the *flota*, a secure fleet of ships that shuttled between port cities, annually stopping at transatlantic hubs such as Havana in Cuba. Through this operation, these hubs became anchors of Spain's imperial commerce.

Few other Atlantic imperial powers, with the exception perhaps of the Portuguese, managed to emulate the complexity of this port city infrastructure. Indeed, by the eighteenth century it was clear that the bureaucracy it generated and the corruption it invited were an unsustainable burden on the profitability of empire. The British favored a more haphazard approach, indicative of the mixed origins of their imperial enterprise. Individual colonial projectors were responsible for founding towns in their colonies, and early on in their histories these places were often more the resort of pirates than the stronghold of the customs officer. Nevertheless, Kingston, New York, Newport, Philadelphia, Boston, and Charleston gradually acquired customs houses, officials, and, eventually, Admiralty Courts, charged with channeling the profits of trade toward the British national treasury.[96]

These cities may have taken a while to acquire the infrastructure of imperial commercial regulation, but privately owned commercial spaces were equally critical to their importance. In each port the waterfront became the epicenter of

[95] Heckscher, *Mercantilism*. [96] Hanna, *Pirate Nests*, 183–249.

commerce. Enriched by Atlantic trade, individual merchants such as William Fishbourn of Philadelphia built outwards and upwards on their wharf lots. The counting houses, weighing rooms, stores, and workshops that they erected were the nerve centers of British Atlantic commerce. Each year, thousands of pounds sterling's worth of goods were loaded and unloaded at these wharves, stimulating growth in associated maritime trades.[97]

By the 1760s, each of these cities had grown to be rich landscapes of transatlantic and coastwise trade that anchored the wealth of the colonies and their value to the empire. They were storehouses of valuable trade goods and repositories of the wealth of leading merchants. When Fishbourn's Wharf on Philadelphia's waterfront burned down in 1730, thousands of pounds' worth of property was lost. Such was its value, that when the Charleston waterfront suffered a devastating fire ten years later, traders received a compensation package from King George II worth 20,000 sterling. Still, this sum was not even ten percent of the estimated quarter million sterling value of the property destroyed.[98]

A large proportion of the goods passing across these wharves were in fact people. It is difficult to overstate the centrality of the slave trade to the commercial importance of these cities. When transatlantic ships arrived in the Americas with their cargoes of suffering and traumatized people, they moored at the wharves of the port city. The sale of people drew planters to the city, adding to its economic growth. Merchants who dealt in people clustered in the city. Across the middle decades of the eighteenth century, the vast riches accumulated from the trade sponsored the construction of lavish townhouse residences, leisure spaces, and places of worship. In other words, profits from the slave trade supported the emergence of rich urban elites.

Not all empires preserved merchant privileges for their subjects. Some of the smaller imperial nations, chiefly the Dutch and the Danish, used a different strategy, which nevertheless was also urban in character. Designating key towns on strategically placed Caribbean islands, such as St Eustatius, as "free ports" they sought to profit by concentrating the trade of goods and people of all nations on their territory. Of course, an imperial monopoly was also impossible in the port cities of West Africa where, as we have seen, Africans themselves dictated the nature of commerce. European visitors were only too aware that they traded there at the pleasure of their hosts.[99]

Understanding that the cityscape was not always a vehicle of commercial monopoly opens the door to deeper considerations of the limits of European

[97] Middleton, "William Fishbourn's 'Misfortune'"; Hart, *Trading Spaces*.
[98] Middleton, "William Fishbourn's 'Misfortune'"; Mulcahy, "'Great Fire' of 1740."
[99] Enthoven, "Abominable Nest of Pirates"; Sparks, *Where the Negroes Are Masters*, 35–67.

economic power at this time. As the limited power of Europeans on the West African coast suggests, port cities did not universally function as the instruments of mercantilism they were intended to be. Rather, they fulfilled their potential as instruments of capital accumulation when they additionally played host to an array of networks operating outside of the European-centered systems designed by the imperialists.

The trading connections of eighteenth-century Havana perfectly exemplify the tangled web of trade that evolved in many Atlantic port cities. A bastion of Spanish power, and a hub of the *flota*, the Cuban town was nevertheless deeply connected to the British and French islands that were in its orbit. When the British laid siege to the town at the end of the Seven Years' War, these myriad trans-imperial networks were laid bare by the crisis. The governor initially failed to identify the invasion, likely because he was so accustomed to British ships appearing on the horizon as part of regular trading relations between Jamaica and Cuba. Both merchants and enslaved Africans lived across imperial boundaries. Many Africans traveled between the British city of Kingston and the Spanish city of Havana as part of a strategy in which they manipulated the economic and legal systems of the two port cities in order to win and preserve their freedom.[100] These multilayered connections were even nurtured by the very merchants who professed loyalty to their monarch in all they did.

Merchant smugglers were a feature of every port city, their global commercial contacts and abundant local knowledge perfectly placing them for profit from the trade in goods across imperial boundaries. Since each city had its own geography and its own interests in particular commodities, smugglers used their specialist knowledge and local connections to confound imperial customs officers. Glasgow merchants connived with Chesapeake planters to underweigh barrels of tobacco, while New York traders kept channels of trade to the French Caribbean open throughout the Seven Years' War to deal across enemy lines. Around Philadelphia and Charleston, merchants identified nearby wharves and villages such as Marcus Hook and Port Royal, where oceangoing ships could moor offshore to unload cargoes of illegal goods into smaller boats that then disappeared into remote coves.[101]

Among the wealthiest residents of port cities, with the power to forge lucrative commercial networks between cities around the Atlantic, merchants were capable of diverting the town from its role as mercantilist hub and remaking it as an inter-imperial entrepôt. When imperial authorities pushed back against these "illegal" activities, the city became the locus of the contest

[100] Schneider, *Occupation of Havana*, 63–112.

[101] Price, "Glasgow, the Tobacco Trade, and the Scottish Customs"; Truxes, *Defying Empire*; Hart, *Trading Spaces*.

between these groups. Conflict unfolded in eighteenth-century Caracas between the Spanish officials of the Caracas Company, established as a monopoly in the cacao trade, and local merchants. The latter deeply resented the Company's intrusion in trading networks that they had established over many decades before the intervention of the imperial center. Spanish officials looked to the city to perform economic control, yet their efforts were contested.[102]

Imperialists built cities not just to connect territories to the metropole but to govern the diverse populations of these territories. In the early modern world, governing urban trade meant protecting the privileges of urban guild members and corporations. In the Atlantic world, such government was both gendered and racialized as it saw European and Creole male officeholders attempt to regulate the participation of women, Africans, and Indigenous people in urban trade. Especially in Spanish, Portuguese, and early Dutch cities, the European guild system was recreated in an effort to reserve trading privileges for white male artisans and tradespeople. European standards of food quality, such as the bread assize, were reintroduced, while much effort was also channeled into licensing the sale of alcohol and regulating provisioning markets.[103]

Such regulatory infrastructure was invariably anchored in the built environment. Customs houses, guild headquarters, and marketplaces featured in towns on both sides of the Atlantic. Even in European towns, the imperial era was an opportunity to "improve" and enlarge these premises, especially in cities that benefited from the Atlantic trade. In Bristol and Liverpool, for example, merchants constructed splendid new exchange buildings. In Glasgow, artisans erected a new Trades House, while the city council laid out new beef and vegetable markets. With the transatlantic hub's wealth and population growing, thanks to the profits of overseas trade, city dwellers devoted resources and energy also to renewing their domestic marketplaces. As part of a shared recommitment to regulating trade, many towns in the Americas soon featured their own market houses, complete with official sets of weights and measures and clerks of the market.[104]

Growing cities were ripe with opportunity for all manner of traders, however. As these traders seized the opportunity to supply city dwellers with essential needs, they became critical to the continued growth of the imperial economy. While skilled artisans could take advantage of demand for their products, men and women in the service trades catered to an expanding population that needed food, drink, and accommodation. Those farmers and dealers living near the city,

[102] Cromwell, *Smugglers' World.*

[103] Bailey, *Art of Colonial Latin America*; Webster, "Masters of the Trade."

[104] Hart, *Trading Spaces.*

meanwhile, enjoyed the marketing opportunities created by urban dwellers who were reliant on them for the necessities of life.

In numerous Atlantic port cities, the people who saw the possibility of making a living from the provision of these services were from diverse ethnic origins. Their diversity created a situation in which Europeans and creoles were reliant on Indigenous, Black, poor white, and sometimes unfree dealers for their daily needs but also regarded them as a source of disorder. Black market women, porters, fishermen, hawkers, and laborers clustered in the marketplace, the streets, and at the wharves. Laboring to feed and service the urban population, they were plainly visible to wealthier white urban dwellers. The result was a constant push and pull between the entrepreneurial activities of this panoply of dealers and European urban rulers who sought to impose on them their version of good order in public space.[105]

Every Atlantic port city relied on the trading activities and skills of men and women and people of African, American, European, and mixed ancestry to operate successfully as a commercial entrepôt. Some colonists desired the maintenance of clear-cut racial hierarchies that separated Indigenous, African, and Europeans while preserving the most skilled and lucrative trades for themselves. Other urbanites realized that their enterprises must be composed of a mixed workforce if they were to be profitable. Therefore, from Boston (Massachusetts) to Buenos Aires, artisan workshops incorporated Africans, Europeans, and Indigenous people working side by side. Wealthy households, meanwhile, were kept running by African cooks, manservants, wet nurses, gardeners, and washerwomen. As skilled carpenters, bricklayers, cabinetmakers, silversmiths, tailors, painters, and more, these workers were then at liberty to deploy their talents for their own profit and satisfaction. In Charleston, South Carolina, European artisans envisaged that enslaved Africans would contribute to the success of their owner-employer's enterprise. For their part, Africans quickly realized that they could monetize their talents for their own support.[106]

The opportunity for personal profit was especially great for African and Indigenous urbanites who had food provisioning skills. In sixteenth-century Potosí, Indigenous women insinuated themselves into the urban economy by supplying bread and chicha (a local alcoholic beverage) to the miners.[107] Through their skill as butchers, many African men became essential to Charleston's meat supply. Some, like the free Black butcher Leander, who

[105] Mangan, *Trading Roles*.

[106] Oliveira, "Gender, Foodstuff Production and Trade"; Burnard, "Slaves and Slavery in Kingston"; Olwell, *Masters, Slaves, and Subjects*.

[107] Mangan, *Trading Roles*.

was a resident of the city in the 1760s, expanded their business to become middlemen and wholesalers of meat, brokering deals between farmers and city consumers. This meat trade also connected the city to the Caribbean, as the exchange of provisions for sugar and molasses grew into a major coastwise commerce between the North American mainland and the islands in the course of the eighteenth century.

In the West African slaving port of Luanda, African women came to play a similar role in the city's manioc flour trade, making a living by dealing in this foodstuff that was essential both to city dwellers and to the provisioning of ships in the slave trade. While Africans and Indigenous people became crucial to these medium-to-large-scale provisioning trades that supplied city people but also consumers in other regions, they were also essential to the smaller-scale networks that kept urbanites in food. In Kingston (Jamaica), Bridgetown (Barbados), and Charleston (South Carolina), provisioning markets were overwhelmingly staffed by men and women of color, who sold food on their own accounts or on behalf of their masters and mistresses. In addition to selling fruit, vegetables, and meat, many also offered prepared dishes such as cooked rice, sweet potatoes, and stews. In the Greater Caribbean, many enslaved people kept their own provision grounds where they grew fruit and vegetables or kept hens, which they offered for sale in the city market.[108]

All around Atlantic port cities, petty merchants of diverse origins also found a niche in the trade of manufactured goods. At tables temporarily erected on the sidewalk, on wharves, in inns, on the street near the marketplace, and in city dwellers' residences, people bought and sold new and second-hand goods (Figure 7). Often, the origin of these wares was uncertain and their exchange was part of an economy that unfolded away from the gaze of urban authorities who, as hard as they tried, failed to contain it. Mexico City's *Baratillo* market, for example, was the hub of dealing among Indigenous, African, and *Mestizo* people, who bought and sold all types of wares there. For the city authorities, however, the *Baratillo* was a source of crime and disorder, subject to sporadic crackdowns by city rulers seeking to regularize urban commerce.[109]

Such a cycle of tension and accommodation, born ultimately of the centrality of these traders to the functioning of the urban economy, was not confined to Mexico City. In Philadelphia, the city corporation complained about the white and Black women huckstering food and trinkets at the margins of the main marketplace, while New York City's authorities repeatedly attempted to break up the interracial networks of traders that operated out of the city's taverns and

[108] Ibid. [109] Konove, "On the Cheap."

Figure 7 "Three Trinket Merchants or Second-Hand Traders," Paramaribo, Suriname (1839).

"Trois marchandes à la toilette ou revendeuses, créole, négresse-créole et cabougle ou africaines," *Slavery Images: A Visual Record of the African Slave Trade and Slave Life in the Early African Diaspora*. www.slaveryimages.org/s/slaveryimages/item/2386.

on its wharves. In Charleston, and to a greater extent in Kingston, Bridgetown, and throughout the Caribbean, Africans and their descendants, both free and enslaved, were almost completely responsible for supplying townspeople with fish and prepared foods. They became, as a result, subjected to sporadic efforts to either close down their trade or confine them to spaces within the city where they might be policed more heavily.

Ultimately, however, these traders endured. Indeed, the historian Andrew Konove has traced the persistence of the *Baratillo* market right through to the twentieth century. The market has remained intact because traders and the city government reached a compromise in which political support is bargained for a lax attitude to the origins of the goods traded there.[110] Such bargains were already common in the early modern Atlantic city. Realizing that closing down the trade altogether would undermine the city's entire provisioning system, colonial elites were constantly vacillating between attempts to confine traders and acceptance that their services were the lifeblood of the city.

In the course of the eighteenth century, the Atlantic's cities evolved into essential trading hubs. Through them, entire imperial trading systems took shape. Yet across the scales of urban trade was a certain tension. Whether international merchant or African huckster, traders were part of constant

[110] Konove, *Black Market Capital*, 171–180.

negotiations – between insiders and outsiders, legal and illegal traders, marginal and necessary dealing. Such was the dynamic in this world of rapidly evolving commercial opportunity.

Sites of Inland Imperial Expansion

Early modern Atlantic cities that became political and economic hubs for European empires were predominantly coastal. But as Europeans explored the interior of the African and American continents in pursuit of promising resources they believed awaited them, they integrated inland towns and cities into the Atlantic system. These places, some indigenous, others founded by European settlers, supported exploratory expeditions, served as commercial outposts or river ports, and oversaw nearby extractive activities. By the late eighteenth century, European settlement in the vast interior of the Americas remained spotty; in Africa, it was mostly a stated goal. Even where European urban settlements existed, the economy and everyday life of these places owed much to the non-European residents who built and animated them. Still, urban sites in the African and American interior helped to extend the reach of Atlantic commerce and power relationships beyond coastlines. Their link to deeper hinterlands further integrated American and African products and people into the expanding Atlantic economy. Like their coastal counterparts, these inland cities cemented Atlantic networks of exchange that ultimately benefited European imperial ambitions.

The development of an early modern Atlantic trade system, particularly the trafficking of enslaved people, affected African patterns of commodity exchange. It did not, however, replace internal dynamics of trade. Away from the coast, people continued to produce agropastoral goods; mine gold, salt, and other minerals; and manufacture items for internal markets. They actively participated in an important trans-Saharan slave trade. This economy relied on complex merchant networks with nodes in key inland cities to move products, people, and credit.[111] From their various enclaves on the Atlantic littoral, Europeans learned about the profitable resources and vibrant trade of the African interior. In his seventeenth-century account of the Gold Coast, the Dutch merchant Pieter de Marees mentioned towns beyond the coast that were more populous and richer in goods and gold than coastal ones. He added that he had heard reports of even larger towns further inland. Indeed, Fante and Hausa city-states, the imperial capital Abomey and Oyo-Ile, among others, were well-urbanized and economically central places that Europeans heard about and whose goods they coveted but which few ever visited. Limited to the coast,

[111] Lovejoy, *Transformations in Slavery*, 45–107.

European traders relied on the commercial brokerage of African towns to access inland riches.[112]

In West Central Africa, where the Portuguese paired their commercial exploits with plans for colonization, the situation was somewhat different. Knowing that the region produced copper, a mineral used as currency in the Indian Ocean trade, Portuguese officers and merchants were eager to control the region's mines. Doing so, they reasoned, required political control over territory. The Portuguese were never able to consolidate political dominance over Central African peoples and resources during the early modern era, though. African kingdoms defended themselves against military attacks and oppressive terms of vassalage. Smaller communities, when threatened, reorganized politically around new figures of authority to protect their autonomy. Moreover, Central African cities remained central to regional networks of trade. But persistent incursions into the region cemented Portuguese trading relationships with various indigenous communities and enabled the establishment of inland fortified outposts. By the eighteenth century, settlements such as Caconda and Ambaca supported regular slave raids and exchanges between the West Central African interior and Portuguese coastal cities.[113]

The pursuit of inland strongholds and towns also characterized European activities in North America. But while mapmakers were quick to represent the region's vast interior as British, French, or Spanish imperial possessions, actual territorial occupation looked much different. The 1763 *A New Map of North America* at least acknowledged an interior that was primarily occupied by Native peoples and only speckled with small, often fortified, European enclaves (Figure 8). The location and longevity of those urban settlements relied on Native peoples and Indigenous towns' desire to trade with their new neighbors.[114]

The town of Santa Fé illustrates the uncertainties that accompanied European urban expansion in the North American interior. Founded along an Indigenous trade route that ran from Mexico City northwards, and surrounded by Native *pueblos* (villages), the town was meant to extend the reach of Spain's political and economic control into northern New Spain. Yet Santa Fé never fully achieved its purpose. Spanish colonial presence in the region was nearly vanquished during the 1680 Pueblo Revolt, when the local Indigenous population besieged and occupied the town. Though the Spanish regained control of Santa Fé, it remained reliant on the resources of New Spain to survive into the

[112] Kea, "City-State Culture on the Gold Coast"; Griffeth, "The Hausa City-States."

[113] Heywood, *Njinga of Angola*, 114–157; Ferreira, *Cross-Cultural Exchange*, 20–51, 58–63; Candido, *An African Slaving Port*, 237–312.

[114] Usner, *Indians, Settlers and Slaves*, 44–76; Hopkins, "A New Landscape," 61–93.

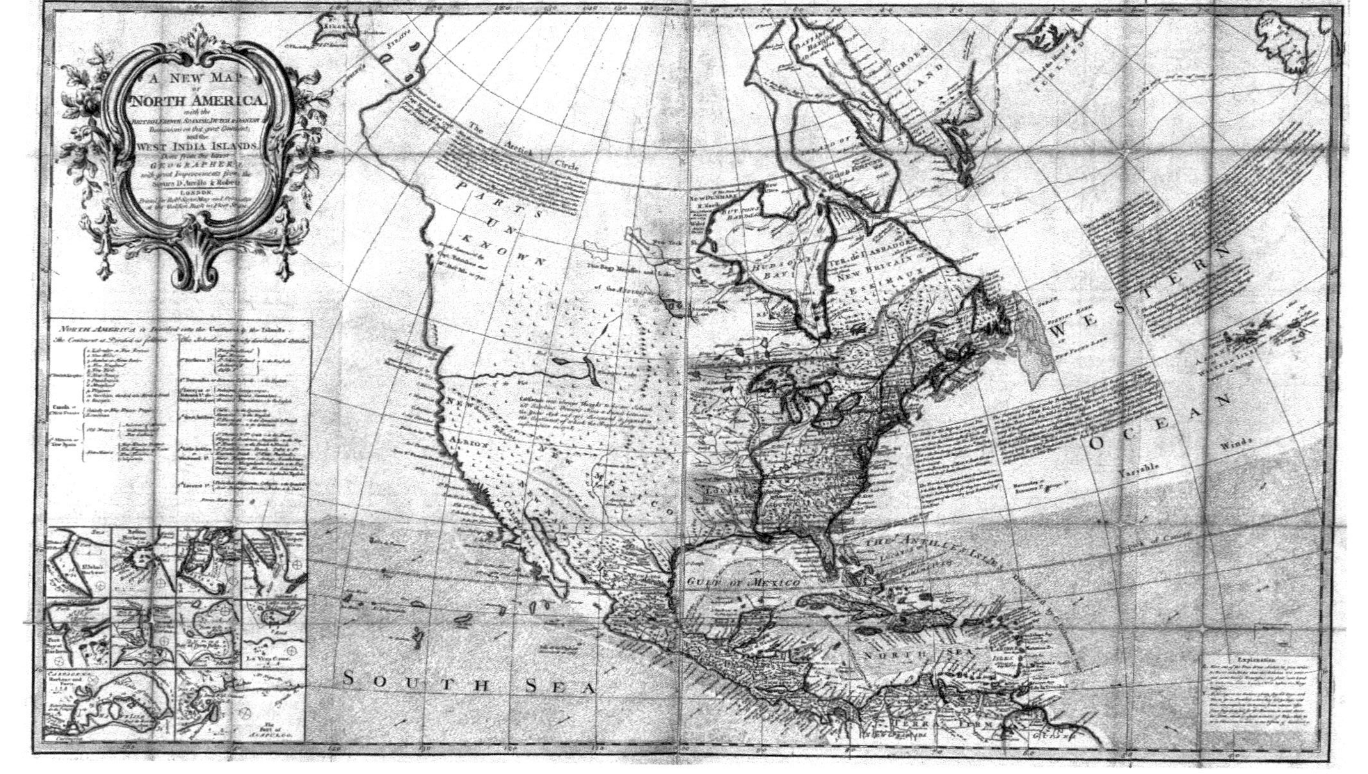

Figure 8 "A New Map of North America, with the British, French, Spanish, Dutch, and Danish Dominions" (1750).

Robert Sayer, Jean Baptiste Bourguignon D' Anville, and Didier Robert De Vaugondy, "A new map of North America, with the British, French, Spanish, Dutch & Danish dominions on that great continent; and the West India Islands" (London: Printed for Robt. Sayer, 1750). Map. Library of Congress, Geography and Map Division. www.loc.gov/item/73696663/.

nineteenth century.[115] Elsewhere in Spanish North America, cities developed around *presidios* (military forts), Catholic missions, and mining sites. Calling them Spanish, though, can be misleading. Though they linked the region to the Spanish empire, their population and material culture were strongly Indigenous. Their everyday activities and relationship with their hinterland, moreover, were often dictated by a Native rather than European political economy.[116]

Among the British and French colonizers of North America, the establishment of inland urban settlements was closely related to the fur trade. European appetite for animal, and particularly beaver, fur animated British and French trade relationships with Indigenous people along the eastern seaboard and as far west as the Mississippi River well into the eighteenth century. The establishment of fortified trading outposts and planned towns in those regions served both to secure access to that valuable resource and to defend one European trading community and their Native allies against threats from the other.[117]

Within the British context, Albany and Carlisle are examples of this urban strategy. An early seventeenth-century Dutch settlement founded upstream on the Hudson River, Albany became part town, part garrison after the British takeover of the region in 1664. Its location and military resources made Albany a crucial staging area for trade and political negotiations with the Iroquois and other Native American groups, and later for Britain's military engagement with the French during the Seven Years' War.[118] Carlisle served similar purposes. Ordered in 1751 by Thomas Penn, the heir of William Penn and one of the proprietors of Pennsylvania, the city would bring English "civilization" to an important trading region west of the Susquehanna River. The city's location was notably near intersecting Indigenous pathways. Its first buildings were taverns, meeting houses, and inns instead of the projected courthouse, jail, and Anglican church. Carlisle clearly catered to local realities rather than Penn's vision of secular and religious order. With the addition of an armory and barracks, Carlisle also became a strategic center for British defense against the French and their Native allies.[119]

French imperial efforts in inland North America also relied on forts and cities to protect and expand fur trading and the Native alliances that sustained it. Settlements founded along the Saint Lawrence, Ohio, and Mississippi Rivers during the seventeenth and eighteenth centuries were often no more than

115 Cruz, *Let There Be Towns*, 19–30; Gutiérrez, *When Jesus Came*, 131–140.

116 Gutiérrez, *When Jesus Came*, 95–149; Williams, "The Evolution of the Presidio"; Hamalainen, *The Comanche Empire*; Corbeil, *The Motions Beneath*.

117 Ingram, *Indians and British Outposts*.

118 Shannon, *Indians and Colonists*, 120–127; Wells, "Global Cities, Glocal Fauna."

119 Ridner, *A Town In-Between*.

a garrison with a handful of families. They nevertheless left a lasting mark on the North American interior. Montreal, Detroit, St. Paul, St. Louis, Natchez, and others made up an urban network that helped the French access, produce, and move profitable commercial goods for the Atlantic trade. After the Seven Years' War and into the nineteenth century, they would – with the exception of Montreal – continue to serve this purpose for other Europeans and their white descendants. While their proximity to major rivers explains in part these cities' chosen location, the presence of Indigenous towns and trading routes were particularly relevant to their placement and development. Like their Spanish counterparts, French North American forts and cities like Natchez were indebted to Native residents and suppliers for their demographic growth and material survival.[120]

Within the Iberian Americas, mining towns stand out for the crucial role they played in early modern global trade and the enrichment of European empires and peoples. Iberian colonial efforts around the Atlantic were driven from the start by the pursuit of gold. Merchants and rulers on the peninsula were well aware of their marginal position within trade networks that reached the rich markets of the Near and Far East. With limited gold and silver reserves, and a lack of competitive commodities, they traded from a position of disadvantage that risked further depletion of their coffers. In the fifteenth century, Portugal, eager to strengthen its commercial and economic standing, set its sights on the gold of North and West Africa. But it was Spain that first gained access to the mines of the Western Hemisphere.[121]

During his first encounters with the Indigenous people of Hispaniola, Columbus and his men noticed the availability of gold. In 1495, he ordered the construction of the fort of Concepción de la Vega, in the island's interior, to support the collection of a gold tribute forced upon the Indigenous population. Spanish settlers were soon after given mining concessions and the right to demand labor tribute from the Natives to expand gold extraction, leading to a period of urban growth at Concepción. By the 1510s and 1520s, the town housed a royal foundry, where the royal fifth (the king's share of the gold output) was processed. It also counted a vibrant urban community of merchants, artisans, and all forms of workers. Though the exhaustion of local gold reserves led to the town's steady decline after the 1540s, archaeological findings reveal a once prosperous and well-supplied urban economy. Importantly, the gold channeled through Concepción financed Spanish campaigns elsewhere in the Caribbean and on the American continent.[122]

---

120 Havard, *Empire et métissages*, 41–111; Gitlin, *The Bourgeois Frontier*, 13–25, 28.

121 Hausberger and Hough-Snee, "Precious Metals in the Americas."

122 Kulstad-González, "Striking It Rich."

Spanish encounters with the sophisticated Indigenous societies of Mesoamerica and the Andes revealed an abundance of mineral riches that astounded many of the early colonists. Not only did the Aztec, Inca, and other Native peoples have large amounts of decorative and ritualistic gold and silver objects – which the invaders promptly smelted and shared with the crown – but they also had knowledge of mines and mining techniques. Indigenous routes and roads leading inland to mining sites and Native towns also proved greatly advantageous to the Spanish, who quickly spread southward and northward from the fallen Aztec capital and into the Andean highlands. Along the way, they founded or took over towns to install municipal governments with the legal authority to grant Spanish settlers the rights to land and labor tribute.[123]

In the arid regions of northern New Spain, the trajectory of towns like Zacatecas and San Luis Potosí was tightly linked to the development of silver mining. Spanish prospectors settled in these towns determined to find ways to extract local riches. But unlike in other areas of New Spain, the neighboring Indigenous population was sparse and indifferent to Spanish presence and activities. If elsewhere the Spanish formed alliances with or coerced Native leaders to conduct campaigns of conquest and collect labor tribute, that was not possible here. Spanish miners and urban residents offered instead wages and accommodated the demands of non-Europeans to secure workers for their mines and to supply and build their towns. Over the course of the seventeenth and eighteenth centuries, northern mining towns attracted a migrant population mostly of Native and African origins that lived and worked alongside Europeans in ways Spanish city planners had not predicted. To be sure, these were not egalitarian urban societies. Miners, elites, and colonial officials worked to protect Spanish privileges and the financial interests of the crown. A vibrant urban economy and readily available silver, however, produced socioeconomic opportunities for non-European townspeople that were not as abundant in other parts of the viceroyalty.[124]

In the Andean region of the viceroyalties of Peru and later New Granada, Spanish settlements and mining activities in the highlands were helped by the existing Indigenous infrastructure, urban network, and system of labor tribute. The Inca road system had supported the movement of people and goods between different climatic zones of economic production and facilitated the collection and allocation of labor tribute. Roads had also enabled disparate Andean communities to move their products and cultivate networks of exchange on their own, boosting local agricultural, mining, and manufacturing

[123] Dym, *From Sovereign Villages*, 3–15.

[124] Bakewell, *Silver Mining and Society*, 41–57; Murillo, *Urban Indians in a Silver City*, 1–52; Corbeil, *The Motions Beneath*, 3–103.

output in the process. Spanish invaders found these features of Inca society highly admirable and co-opted them to serve their own imperial goals.[125] Newly founded or occupied towns – including *reducciones* for resettled Indigenous populations – further contributed to Spain's imperial ambitions. With their churches, cabildos, and elite houses, Popayan, Tunja, (Santafé de) Antioquia, among others, brought European religion, laws, and power to densely populated highland regions. The royal mint and *audiencia* (high court) in Bogotá, the seat of the viceroyalty, directed wealth generated through gold, silver, and emerald mining toward Spain and the broader Atlantic economy.[126]

The most famous Spanish colonial mining town was of course the city of Potosí. Founded in 1545 in the highlands of the viceroyalty of Peru (present-day Bolivia), Potosí supported the extraction of unimaginable amounts of silver from the imposing *cerro* (hill) that loomed over it. The impact of its silver on global trade turned Potosí into the stuff of legend. Like elsewhere in Spanish South America, mining in Potosí relied heavily on forced Indigenous labor, mobilized through the brutal labor tribute system the Spanish enforced. The needs and promises of an urban economy fueled by silver also attracted diverse groups of European settlers, Indigenous migrants, and trafficked enslaved Africans, making Potosí more populous than most European cities by the 1570s. With its Indigenous market women, African bakers, and artisans and urban entrepreneurs of diverse origins, the city epitomized the complex socio-economic environment of Atlantic mining towns. Importantly, Potosí is a reminder that cities which helped to build the wealth that sustained European empires were shaped by the diverse groups of people who inhabited them.[127]

In the Portuguese colony of Brazil, the discovery of gold and the ensuing development of mining towns happened much later than in the Spanish Americas. Throughout the sixteenth and seventeenth centuries, the main economic activity driving inland expeditions was slave raids targeted at Indigenous villages, which hardly incentivized long-term settlements. Dense forests, Indigenous resistance, and the absence of well-worn routes further contributed to a predominantly coastal pattern of colonization. This reality changed dramatically, however, at the turn of the eighteenth century, when alluvial gold was found in abundance in the southeastern backlands of the colony. News of the

[125] Ramirez, *To Feed and to Be Fed*, 1, 34–35; Garrido, "Rethinking Imperial Infrastructure"; Mumford, *Vertical Empire*, 88.

[126] McFarlane, *Columbia before Independence*, 16–20, 71–98; Díaz, *Esclavitud, región y ciudad*, 23–36; Lane, *Colour of Paradise*.

[127] Mangan, *Trading Roles*, 76–105; Voigt, *Spectacular Wealth*, 87–120; Lane, *Potosi*, 1–19, 92–116.

discovery quickly attracted migrants from various parts of Brazil and from Portugal. Miners, a rapidly rising population of enslaved African workers, merchants, artisans, and others formed numerous small hamlets close to mining sites. Disputes over land and political authority and unrest among the enslaved soon produced violent confrontations, leading imperial officials to act quickly. By the 1720s, the mining district was made into its own captaincy and several towns were founded by royal order.[128]

The creation of the captaincy of Minas Gerais followed the basic blueprint Portugal had used to secure coastal Brazil. A newly appointed captain general, a high court, and a military force were all put in place to promote Portuguese interests. Incorporated royal towns, moreover, with their municipal councils of elected officials, were charged with processing the royal fifth and enforcing Portuguese law, justice, and political order. The rights and privileges afforded to the white members of those governing bodies bound their priorities to those of the crown, forging loyal Portuguese vassals in the colonial backlands.[129] Minas Gerais's towns also witnessed the economic dynamism of Africans and their descendants. These non-white townspeople found ways to leverage their work and relevance to the mining and urban economy into earnings and even freedom from slavery. Their social and cultural activities, as well as leadership in their own *irmandades* (religious associations), shaped much of the urban experience in the mining region.[130] The mining towns of Brazil, like Potosí and others, enriched the Iberian empires and injected extraordinary amounts of bullion into the global economy, helping to explain European economic power in the early modern period. The prominence of Africans and African descendants within these urban societies invites us to reconsider, however, the primacy of Europe in the development of the Atlantic world.

The scantiness of European-founded towns and cities and the limited size of European urban enclaves in the interior of Africa and the Americas highlight the limits of European imperial reach around the Atlantic. The crucial role non-European urban actors played in sustaining inland activities that fed the Atlantic economy, moreover, underscores the need for research that considers seriously their importance to early modern urban history. Still, the relationship between inland Atlantic urban sites and profitable industries – fur trading, slave trafficking, and gold and silver mining in particular – explains the incremental shift in the balance of power that characterized the early modern Atlantic. The wealth and the capital these industries generated may have favored Indigenous

[128] Romero, *Paulistas e Emboabas*; Andrade, *A invenção das Minas Gerais*; Fonseca, *Arraiais e Vilas*, 51–167.
[129] Gouvêa, "Redes de poder na América portuguesa"; Bicalho, *A cidade e o império*, 163–181.
[130] Dantas, *Black Townsmen*, 11–96; Dantas, "Une autre lecture des fondations urbaines."

Africans and Americans, transplanted and enslaved Africans, and their descendants to some extent. But they ultimately strengthened the power of Europeans and their descendants within a world economic system that was becoming truly global.

Conclusion

By the mid-eighteenth century, the Atlantic world was a well-connected space. Human activities in one corner of that world shaped in tangible ways the activities and everyday lives of people across continental and oceanic expanses. Port cities, inland towns, and even modest villages did much of that connective work. Their governing bodies and religious leaders dictated rules and customary practices that regulated so many of these connections. Their institutions enforced those rules, while in their public squares the violent consequences suffered by those who challenged them were on display. Their wharves, warehouses, and markets facilitated the trade that supplied the needs and selectively enriched much of Europe, African, and the Americas. Yet these urban places were not neutral agents in the development of Atlantic exchanges. As they facilitated the transoceanic movement of people, goods, and ideas, they also helped to direct the flow of wealth and power disproportionately toward European monarchs and their white subjects. In this sense, they became engines of empire for Europe.

That is not to say, however, that Europeans achieved absolute control over the early modern Atlantic world. Cities may have been a technology of empire, but they were hardly a foolproof tool for social engineering compliance with the expectations of European rulers and elites. Atlantic exchanges generated a range of opportunities for those seeking to participate in new forms of trade, access novel means of wealth, and challenge the status quo. Urban practices, places, and institutions enabled those efforts while also mediating and normalizing their outcomes. Though riddled with the hierarchical inequalities of the early modern era, Atlantic cities were nevertheless more accommodating than plantation or rural societies to the ambitions of non-elites and non-Europeans. Those who found ways to mobilize resources such as fur, precious metals, or enslaved human beings, and to meet emerging demands for goods, labor, political leadership, or spiritual guidance, were able to carve a place of relevance for themselves. On their own, cities did not bring about European or white supremacy. But as those who inhabited or transacted within them operated under the aegis of European urban institutions and networks to advance their interests, they did not challenge the overall prominence of white Europeans within the Atlantic system. At least not for much of the early modern era.

As the eighteenth century progressed, the Atlantic world became a more complex place. Population growth and dispersal in the Americas, European imperial wars, and changing geopolitics in Africa tested the strengths of urban institutions that had aimed to produce continuity within the Atlantic space and direct the flow of wealth and power. A petition drafted in 1761 by the inhabitants of the town of Reading to the Pennsylvania legislators hints at the misgivings even small and remote urban places had about the constraints these institutions imposed. Complaining that their then current system of government limited the authority inland cities were capable of wielding, the petitioners wrote that "for Want of Power to make By-Laws, or other Regulations" they could not provide "for the Government of so many People living together." As a result, they claimed, the situation was "dangerous in many places."[131] The urban network that Europeans strove to craft in order to shape the political and economic fabric of the Atlantic world was breaking at the seams. Through those openings, urban residents glimpsed possible new directions for the flow of power, opportunity, and wealth.

4 Cities and Atlantic Freedoms

The book *Saint-Domingue, ou Histoire de ses Revolutions*, published in 1815, wastes no time in depicting for its readers the horrors white settler colonists experienced during the Haitian Revolution. Its frontispiece shows the city of Cap Français burning in the background while its white residents attempt to escape a violent attack by Black men armed with makeshift weapons (Figure 9). The well-dressed and shoe-wearing white figures in the foreground contrast with the barefoot, shoddy-dressed, and most likely enslaved Black man chasing them. Yet any sympathy a reader might feel for his plight is eroded by the pleading gestures of his potential victims, among whom are vulnerable elderly people and young children. The book's subtitle, moreover, minces no words. It claims to recount the divisions, troubles, ravages, deaths, fires, devastations, and massacres that happened on the island after 1789. The spectacle of non-Europeans destroying the lives, property, and urban creations of white imperialists terrified the white Atlantic world. Indeed, the Haitian Revolution became a cautionary tale, encouraging racial oppression in subsequent decades. Yet the same words could have been used to describe most other events from the "Age of Revolution," the era from the 1760s to the 1850s that was first given coherence by Eric Hobsbawm.[132] During these decades of upheaval across the Atlantic world, imperial and royal authority were widely rejected and the urban symbols of their power targeted by violent mobs. In their stead, people

[131] Pearl, *Conceived in Crisis*, 60–63. [132] Hobsbawm, *Age of Revolution*.

Figure 9 "Burning of Cap. General Revolt of the Negroes. Massacre of the Whites" (1815).

"Incendie du Cap. Révolte général des Nègres. Massacre des Blancs," *Saint-Domingue, ou Histoire des ses révolutions* (Paris: chez Tiger, imprimeur-libraire, [1815?]). The Library Company of Philadelphia, Books & Other Texts, Rare Am 1815 Sai 66601.D. https://digital.librarycompany.org/islandora/object/Islandora%3A2721.

sought governments who were answerable to their demands and friendly to their pursuit of "liberty."

During this tumultuous era, clashes between colonists and colonial powers, between monarchs and their subjects, culminated in the American, French, and Haitian Revolutions, Islamic wars of expansion in West Africa, and the wars of independence in South America. These conflicts were almost always the product of political tensions or dissent. They also owed much to frustrations and resentment over the unequal distribution of wealth and power around the Atlantic world. Those inequalities were particularly on display in cities, where for much of the early modern period urban residents had pursued political and economic autonomy. The wars and economic crises of the eighteenth century undermined those pursuits, however, while new ideological currents upped the stakes, fueling these revolutionary movements. Every revolution was both a rural and an urban affair, yet towns often fomented uprisings and witnessed the battles for supremacy that ensued.

Many Atlantic cities had reached new heights in size, wealth, and complexity by the late eighteenth century. Some cities had of course been very large all along – London, Mexico City, and Paris had tens (and even hundreds) of thousands of inhabitants from the 1500s onwards. Joining them were numerous towns that were growing exponentially. Rio de Janeiro was home to 24,000 inhabitants in 1749 and 113,000 in 1821. Philadelphia had grown from a small town of a few thousand people in the early eighteenth century to a metropolis of some 155,000 in 1830. Without exception, larger populations translated into greater social, racial, and economic diversity, a diversity that ensured people with differing ideas about city life would be gathered together in close proximity.

The role of the expanding city in this revolutionary age was multifaceted. As cultural and political entrepôts, they nurtured the ideological foundations of revolutionary movements. As centers of communication and print, they were well equipped to spread these ideas. As the home of rich and poor, of white and Black people, of colonial elites and imperial officials, the revolutionary-era city was itself primed to become an engine of conflict. As conflict played out in various cities connected by the Atlantic, old disputes over socioeconomic and racial inequalities broke out in familiar urban spaces recast in the new language of this era. In the Americas, colonial cities that had supported imperial projects became bulwarks of emerging national ones. And throughout the Atlantic, the meaning and uses of urban spaces shifted and were reappropriated by distinct political groups eager to claim political and economic gains for themselves.

The Discontented City

Cities imported European institutions of secular and religious power to the Americas. Although not completely successful in achieving the wished-for levels of mastery among the local population, they had nevertheless been successful at circulating governing structures and customs around the Atlantic. From the 1600s onward, urban governments in Europe and the Americas experienced a period of bureaucratic expansion that provided plentiful opportunities for white non-elite citizens to participate in politics. By the eighteenth century, white men in towns around the Atlantic were coalescing into political factions. These factions claimed rights and power in urban government – sometimes peacefully and sometimes more violently, sometimes in print and sometimes through direct action. Their actions around the Atlantic reveal the growing city as a promoter of popular political action wherever it arose. Until the 1760s, however, protest remained localized and did not aim for an overthrow of the existing monarchical order.

The city's political role expanded first of all when European institutions of urban government were successfully replicated around the Atlantic – and especially in the Americas and the Caribbean. Chief among these institutions were craft guilds, municipal councils, and city corporations, organizations that the Spanish and the Portuguese replicated to varying degrees. The British were less successful in this respect – mostly because of their more eclectic modes of colonization – but nevertheless a number of cities chose to create such bodies. Through these institutions, white men of middling means gained political experience and, often, a belief that they had the right to participate in government.[133]

In Spanish America, metropolitan ideas of citizenship had made their way across the Atlantic to shape the urban political community. *Vecinidad* – or urban citizenship – was acquired through active participation in the urban community. Since they were barred from practicing citizenly duties, immigrants and foreigners might be excluded from this status. Hence, citizens of Quito sought to protect urban political and economic privileges from those who lived in surrounding rural areas and were thus presumed not to work for the benefit of the urban community. Spanish merchants, on the other hand, set about protecting their trading monopoly from interlopers who were not resident townsmen. Citizens of Spanish origin also worked to protect their status in the face of challenges from Indigenous and Black inhabitants.[134]

The effectiveness of the cabildo as a governing entity of both urban and rural space was a foundation of imperial governance and, increasingly, a key location in which white men developed an idea of themselves as rights-bearing citizens. Through their work on the town council, they took responsibility for urban law and order and also for the governance of the surrounding countryside. With the Bourbon reforms of the 1740s onward, cabildos then assumed even greater importance for white colonists, who turned to them as local powerbases in the face of efforts by Spain's new dynasty to assert greater bureaucratic control over their American territories.[135]

In Anglo-Atlantic cities, townsmen encountered multiple new opportunities for participation in local politics. When they grew in population and size, British cities expanded their governments, enlarging existing institutions and adding new ones. By the 1730s, the city council of the Scottish port town of Glasgow faced a rapidly growing city and economy thanks to the opportunities generated by the Atlantic trade. It responded by establishing a new deepwater port (Port Glasgow), relocating and rebuilding the marketplaces where grains, beef, and vegetables were sold, and erecting a splendid new Trades House, where the city's craft guilds were headquartered.[136] The construction and regulation of these new spaces provided a larger number of townsmen with the opportunity to become active citizens.

133 Johnson, *Workshop of Revolution*, 117–148; Nash, *Urban Crucible*, 95; Middleton, *From Privileges to Rights*, 96–130.
134 Kinsbruner, *Independence in Spanish America*, 27–32; Herzog, *Defining Nations*.
135 Kinsbruner, *Independence in Spanish America*.
136 Hart, *Trading Spaces*.

The era also witnessed the emergence of a rich urban voluntary culture among free white men. Social, charitable, and cultural clubs were established in large quantities. In Philadelphia and Bristol, men founded hospitals and almshouses that would provide for the sick and the "deserving poor" through donations of virtuous citizens. In most North American cities, men of particular ethnic origins came together to form clubs that could create a support network in their new home through business contacts, social opportunities, and, sometimes, financial assistance. The St Andrew's Society was for Scots, St George's for the English, and the German Society for those who had emigrated from the continent. Other groups of townsmen gathered as the St Cecilia's Society to host concerts for urban music-lovers. While very different in their ambitions, these voluntary societies all served to develop the corporate sensibilities of their members, who were taught to see themselves as the town's leading citizens with a fundamental role in maintaining the health of the body politic.[137]

Because these clubs concerned themselves with the social fabric and order of the city, they also represented an enlargement of urban governance. Further expansion occurred when British colonists chose to replicate familiar institutions of political power in their growing American cities. In Philadelphia, the establishment of a city corporation in 1701 created an array of positions for the aspirational citizen, including mayor and common councilman. When the English seized New Amsterdam from the Dutch in 1664, they inherited an extensive infrastructure of urban governance, including trade guilds, a mayor, and a common council, with their authority bolstered by their own court systems. Boston and other New England towns were ruled by their selectmen, who were closely linked to the church.[138]

Not every colonial city harbored such abundant political opportunity for the enthusiastic citizen. Caribbean towns such as Kingston (Jamaica) and Bridgetown (Barbados) remained without their own city governments in this era. Charleston was not incorporated until 1783, meaning that there were fewer possibilities for men seeking a piece of the local civic action. This did not translate into a total exclusion for men keen to make their mark on the cityscape, however. By mid-century, both Charleston and its Caribbean counterparts had a number of urban "commissions," designed to oversee order and "improvement" in the streets, at the wharves, on the fortifications, and in the marketplace. What is more, reliance on such bodies in these colonial cities mirrored a major rise in their popularity in England, where Julian Hoppit has tracked an

[137] Clark, *British Clubs and Societies*; Wilson, "Urban Culture and Political Activism in Hanoverian England"; Paul, "Credit and Ethnicity in the Urban Atlantic World."

[138] Middleton, *From Privileges to Rights*; Roney, *Governed by a Spirit*, 38–58; Levy, *Town Born*, 125–152.

exponential increase in the creation of so-called improvement commissions, the vast majority of which were preoccupied with urban infrastructure.[139] Sanctioned by an Act of Parliament, these commissions were dedicated to the creation of specific urban infrastructure, such as street lighting. Participation in them opened up urban governance to a new array of white male citizens.

In the century before 1750, city governance proved to be an Atlantic-wide nursery of enthusiastic citizens whose political consciousness was honed through the regulation of their immediate, urban surroundings. Closely tied to specific city environments, however, this consciousness remained profoundly parochial for the first part of the eighteenth century. Nevertheless, it increasingly formed the basis of explosions of local and national protest that punctured the day-to-day business of urban rulership. While these protests did not threaten to amalgamate into any transnational movements, or threaten to topple royal authority, they did become visibly more frequent as the eighteenth century progressed.

Cities nurtured many possibilities for white male citizens to articulate and refine their political opinions. As a city government, through participation in celebrations, or by protesting in the streets, non-elite men carved new channels of political expression, challenging ensconced ruling elites. In doing so, they made the growing Atlantic city the chief vehicle of political protest. Not all cities offered the same array of opportunities, however. The levels of dissent tolerated by monarchs varied widely, as did the willingness of their regional and colonial representatives to entertain disagreement with official policy. In the English-speaking Atlantic world, the urban press became a core vehicle of political expression. This outlet was best developed for this purpose thanks to the lapsing of censorship laws at the end of the seventeenth century. Such laws remained in place in the French-, Spanish-, and Portuguese-speaking worlds, stymying the emergence of a similarly lively world of political print.

Printing presses had become ubiquitous in many larger and medium-sized English-speaking towns by the middle of the eighteenth century. With the lack of prepublication censorship, printers were free to turn out newspapers, pamphlets, and broadsides containing the opinions and agendas of local politics. From Aberdeen to Salisbury in Britain, and from Boston to Bridgetown in America, cohorts of citizens gradually embraced print as the means by which they might articulate and refine their views of local issues. Since these printed materials were usually available in urban taverns and coffeehouses, as well as by individual subscription, they rapidly became promoters of public debate.[140]

[139] Hoppit, "Patterns of Parliamentary Legislation."

[140] Ferdinand, *Benjamin Collins and the Provincial Newspaper Trade*, 62–94; Wilson, *Sense of the People*, 27–83.

On both sides of the British Atlantic, multiple incidents reveal how print sponsored the development of white male civic consciousness among non-elites. In 1730s Philadelphia, Benjamin Franklin put his *Pennsylvania Gazette* in the service of the debate between the city council and the city's butchers and tanners over responsibility for water pollution caused by their trades. Through newspaper articles and in meetings of the council, Philadelphians became participants in questions of private enterprise and the public good, of civic duty and personal liberty.[141]

While such debates may seem second nature to inhabitants of the twenty-first-century city, they were a novelty in a political culture that was only beginning to embrace the possibility of dissent and the potential for social inferiors to contest the rule of their superiors. In the context of the colonial city, this was easier than it was in the British urban environment. By 1735, colonial lawyers had already enjoyed a victory for press freedom when they won the libel case brought by the New York governor William Cosby against the newspaper editor John Peter Zenger. Partisan print that displayed no qualms about disagreeing with the government became a regular feature of the colonial American press over the middle of the eighteenth century.[142]

Britain's urban elites had a tougher time accepting the objections of their inferiors, but this did not mean that a city's emerging middle classes were about to stop expressing them. The city of Durham's religious elites were horrified when, in the 1750s, citizens began placing articles in the newspapers of nearby Newcastle upon Tyne accusing them of fraudulently increasing their power over town affairs. This power struggle had actually been underway for more than a century, but the efforts of townsmen to garner popular support for their cause in the press was a new development and represented a broadening of a dispute that had previously been conducted behind closed doors.[143]

The effort to popularize a political cause through the press was reminiscent of many others that historians have traced in the English-speaking print of this era. Both in Britain and in its American colonies, newspapers began to print letters, essays, and news reports that furthered the agendas of varied constituencies of the urban body politic. Celebrations of imperial victories, such as that of Admiral Vernon against the Spanish at Portobello in 1739, complaints about the decisions of urban governments, and popular objections to the political decisions made in Whitehall, all gained traction through their discussion in the local newspaper. This was how Whig and Tory allegiances extended beyond London and into the English provinces.

141 Finger, *Contagious City*, 70–73. 142 Olsen, "Zenger Case Revisited."
143 Hart, *Trading Spaces*, 147–149.

These newspapers also frequently published reports of crowd actions that were common in growing towns of this era and were frequently centered in city spaces. A rise in food riots, the Jacobite Uprisings of 1715 and 1745, protests against new taxes such as the Cider Duties of 1763, and industrial action, all received press coverage by writers who were quite willing to express partisan opinions. Such articles created at least regional awareness of popular political issues. In the wake of the new cider tax, a combination of print and popular protest in the towns of southwest England – the center of cider production – resulted in the duty's revocation. The victory of the protestors was duly celebrated in the newspapers.[144]

Outside of the English-speaking Atlantic, the press was not free enough, and provincial newspapers were not numerous enough, for the written word and direct action to mutually encourage the rise in urban political dispute. Nevertheless, as a self-identified body of rights-bearing citizens, Spanish-speaking urban dwellers showed themselves fully capable of rising up in protest when they felt their rights to be under threat from royal decisions. The king's desire to increase income from the *quinto* – the tax on gold – prompted armed resistance in the Brazilian town of Vila Rica in 1720. In 1749, some 500 citizens of Caracas came out to protest against the efforts of the Spanish crown to monopolize the cocoa trade. Led by Juan Francisco de Leon, they gathered in the central plaza, filled with anger that their right to freely trade this commodity was threatened by a new royal monopoly. A quarter of a century later, the citizens of Quito would launch an equally vociferous protest when the viceroy proposed to raise the tax rates on *aguardiente*, a sugar cane brandy. Beginning with petitions from elites arguing that it was their right to decide this tax, the protest escalated into an uprising when poorer white and Indigenous urbanites seized the opportunity to demonstrate their dissatisfaction with those very elites.[145]

Whether they were petitioning against the tax on sugar cane brandy in Quito or the duty on cider in Taunton, Atlantic world city dwellers shared an experience in which urban politics was becoming more lively and more accessible to a larger swathe of the white male population. The growing urban ecosystem, with its ever-larger population of non-elite free white men, set in motion these shifts by giving the means and the cause of popular opposition to elite and royal government. Generally, the issues on which they protested were local in character. Yet there were already some instances by the 1760s in which regional movements – centered on clusters of towns and cities – had taken shape.

---

[144] Randall and Charlesworth, *Market Culture and Popular Protest*, 74–75.

[145] Cromwell, *Smugglers' World*; Kinsbruner, *Independence in Spanish America*, 27–32.

> People flock into cities; love to receive and communicate knowledge; to show their wit or their breeding; their taste in conversation or living, in clothes or furniture . . . both sexes meet in an easy and sociable manner; and the tempers of men, as well as their behavior, refine apace . . . they must feel an increase in humanity from the very habit of conversing together.

So claimed Scottish Enlightenment thinker David Hume in 1752.[146] In no case, however, did protestors fundamentally question the monarchical order. Rather, this was a process through which a growing urban population nurtured politically active men looking to take on their duties as citizens and claim the rights and liberties that were due to them as such.

Urban Struggles against the Atlantic Racial Order

In the same manner that they fomented white political ambitions, Atlantic cities fueled the aspirations of Africans, Native Americans, and their descendants. To be sure, the early modern urban Atlantic produced socio-racial differentiation that enforced white European entitlement to wealth and power and Native American and African subordination. Black men, women, and children were held in slavery in the forts and warehouses of port towns. Indigenous peoples were forced to resettle in Spanish *reducciones* or Puritan praying towns. Non-European servants worked and shared confining living quarters in the ground floors, kitchens, and backhouses of urban elite households. At times, however, non-Europeans successfully co-opted the various urban institutions and spaces that promoted this socio-racial order to challenge their subordination.

African and Indigenous American people, for example, managed to participate in urban economies on their own terms by using urban gardens, market-spaces, and street corners to supply local demands for food and services. They leveraged cities' desire for order and civility to mobilize against their tormentors the very judicial system and governing bodies that regularly sought to control them. When pushed, they attacked, occupied, and temporarily repurposed urban symbols of European power such as fortifications, squares, public buildings, and churches. In short, through their efforts to claim the city and redirect its resources and promises, Africans, Indigenous Americans, and their descendants articulated a broader vision of Atlantic freedom.

Throughout the early modern Atlantic world, urban settlements from the coastal villages of West Africa to the inland mining towns of South America mediated encounters and exchanges between Europeans, Africans, and Indigenous Americans. In these places, townspeople traded, negotiated political alliances, and forged tenuous consensus over the terms of their engagement with

[146] Hume, "Of Refinement of the Arts."

one another. At times, however, their different expectations for these emerging relationships caused violent confrontations. In Africa and the Americas, a few of these episodes arose because of disruptions European encroachment caused to Indigenous African or American communities. By the late seventeenth and eighteenth centuries, some also reflected non-European efforts to claim Atlantic opportunities and freedoms for themselves.

European forts and factories in West and Central Africa, for instance, were often the targets of violent attacks when the commercial and political relationships they mediated soured. Towns like Saint Louis, in Senegal, and Luanda, in Angola, saw their share of violence. These places operated through an often uneasy alliance between local African elites and foreign European traders. At the best of times their business together, notably the slave trade, helped to empower the former and enrich the later. But occasionally it threatened the economic interests and political sovereignty of European rivals and African peoples who then pursued the strategic destruction of these places to defend their priorities. During the eighteenth century, regional and imperial disputes similarly caused violent conflicts in the coastal towns of the Gold Coast and Bight of Biafra. These towns had become central to the trafficking in enslaved people that powered the Atlantic economic system. As a result, they were viewed as desirable assets to be conquered or an enemy strength to be neutralized.[147]

In the Americas, towns and cities were sometimes turned into battlefields in response to European colonial violence. Two early episodes unfolded in Tenochtitlán and in Cuzco. In 1520, Tenochca warriors attacked the Spanish who were stationed in the Aztec capital. After days of battle, Aztec forces pushed the Spanish out, causing two-thirds to die during the tumultuous retreat – many drowned in the city's canals and lake. A year later, strengthened by the support of their Native allies and equipped with boats and mobile bridges, the Spanish lay siege to and attacked the city. Cortés and his men's brutal treatment of the survivors and of the city itself in the aftermath of the Aztec defeat cemented the Spanish rise to power in the region.[148] Nearly two decades later, in 1536, another war was underway in the Andes. After escaping his predicament as a puppet ruler of the Spanish in Cuzco, Manco Inca mobilized a large army to expel the Spanish from the Inca capital and to destroy the town of Lima. Despite their initial success, the Inca army was eventually forced to retreat by

[147] Lovejoy, *Transformations in Slavery*, 66–87; Vidal, *Mazagão*, 15–50; Sparks, *The Two Princes*, 10–32; Shumway, *The Fante*, 88–131; Candido, *An African Slaving Port*, 31–76; Heywood, *Njinga of Angola*, 133–157; Searing, "The Seven Years' War in West Africa."

[148] Townsend, *Malintzin's Choices*, 98–125.

Spanish forces and their Native allies. Inca towns played an important role in that retreat and the survival of a diminished Inca empire until 1572.[149]

Towns were also the target of Indigenous resistance against colonization in North America. The first English settlements of Roanoke and Jamestown, as well as English and praying towns in Massachusetts, were damaged or destroyed by the Powhatan and Wampanoag, respectively. Santa Fé, the capital of the Spanish colonial province of Nuevo Mexico, was attacked and occupied by the surrounding Pueblo *Indios* (as Indigenous peoples were termed). Native American rejection of their material, labor, and physical exploitation by European colonizers culminated in these seventeenth-century assaults against the towns that helped to systematize that exploitation. The English and Spanish termed these actions rebellions or revolts, thus characterizing them as criminal and politically illegitimate. Continued European military and financial investment in these colonial projects, moreover, often vanquished these Indigenous assertions of sovereignty. Still, the material and human costs they inflicted, and the threat they posed to European authority, encouraged changes to colonial policies and practices. Indigenous people faced a growing asymmetry of power in their dealings with European Atlantic empires, but their presence and voice were never erased.[150]

Late seventeenth- and eighteenth-century cities and towns in the Americas, by then stable features of European colonization, continued to witness violent confrontations between local populations. The hierarchy of power in these urban societies and their hinterland, enforced by municipal governments, courts, and armed militias, favored Europeans and their white descendants. Yet, as much as the people in power hoped to control those they deemed subordinates, violent rejection of that subjugation was an ever-present threat. That threat materialized in Mexico City in 1692, a year when failed harvests and the colonial government's mismanagement of food prices condemned the mainly Indigenous and *Mestizo* urban poor to a severe hunger crisis. Simmering anger boiled over into a riot when a small mob trying to get justice for a dying Indigenous woman was forcefully turned away from the diocese, the viceroy's palace, and the cabildo. The crowd in the city's main square quickly joined in the protest, calling for the death of Spanish officials and attacking the buildings that housed them. Long after the riot was quelled, the damaged facade of the viceregal palace and other buildings remained as a testament to the destruction exploited urban residents could cause if pushed too far (Figure 10).[151]

[149] Flickema, "The Siege of Cuzco"; Martinez, "La Rebelión de Manco Inka."
[150] Kupperman, *Roanoke*; Horn, *A Brave and Cunning Prince*; Gutiérrez, *When Jesus Came*.
[151] Haslip-Viera, "The Underclass"; Cope, *The Limits of Racial Domination*, 125–160.

Figure 10 Detail of "Vista de la Plaza Mayor de la Ciudad de México" by Cristóbal de Villalpando showing damages to the viceregal palace (1695). A photograph of this painting appears on the title page of Kagan, *Urban Images*. There is also a copy on https://commons.wikimedia.org/wiki/File:Vista_de_la_Plaza_Mayor_de_la_Ciudad_de_M%C3%A9xico_-_Cristobal_de_Villalpando.jpg.

Fears of an uprising by the large enslaved African and African descendant populations that inhabited so many cities throughout the Americas also fed white urban anxieties. Whether in Havana (Cuba), Cartagena (Colombia), New York, Salvador (Bahia), or the mining towns of South America, enslaved people regularly resorted to violence to resist or escape the brutality of slavery. Attacks on enslavers and other urban residents, arson, destruction of property, flight, and the willingness to take up arms to resist recapture were some of the behaviors that scared townspeople and white officials. These events invariably encouraged legislation and policing that criminalized almost any Black rejection of exploitation and humiliation.[152] Despite the cruelty of the punishments they received, enslaved people nevertheless persistently challenged the practice of slavery and its racial logic.

Urban communities proved to be an important resource for Black people's pursuit of freedom from the violence of slavery. To be sure, coordinated or large urban slave revolts were rare. The risks were too great and the backlash too swift and severe. Much more common was the rejection of slavery by individuals or small groups through flight. Enslaved people's efforts to seek out cities where they could claim freedom of movement, association, and economic agency are well documented in the numerous runaway ads published in the newspapers of

152 Schneider, *Occupation of Havana*, 41–42; Landers, "The African Landscape of Seventeenth-Century Cartagena"; Lepore, *New York Burning*; Reis, *Slave Rebellion in Brazil*, 3–72; Anastasia, *Vassalos Rebeldes*, 123–136; Sharples, *The World That Fear Made*, 20–104.

British North America and, later, the United States.[153] The same practice was common throughout the Americas. The urban demand for labor, urban residents' willingness to harbor escapees, and the access cities – particularly ports – afforded to other places of refuge made urban places attractive to those escaping slavery.[154] In time, towns and cities became known as places where Black hope for freedom could be realized.[155]

Escaped enslaved people in South America, the Caribbean, and to a lesser extent North America did more than seek their freedom in existing towns and cities. Some established their own villages or encampments, known as *quilombos*, *palenques*, and maroons. These places were similar to early European colonial urban settlements, or indeed African villages, with populations that could reach the several hundreds.[156] The plan of the *quilombo* Buraco do Tatu from Bahia, Brazil, drawn by one of its attackers, showed houses, a fountain, a square, vegetable gardens, and various protective trenches reinforced with stakes.[157] Maroon towns and villages often traded with neighboring communities, or resorted to looting, to secure supplies. Unlike European or indigenous African villages, however, they could not count on existing urban commercial networks to survive. Considered a threat to the slave order, they were shown little tolerance and were aggressively persecuted. Nevertheless, some became strong enough that colonial governments were forced to recognize their right to exist, as was the case in Jamaica and Suriname.[158] Moreover, as one frustrated town councillor in Minas Gerais lamented, even when one *quilombo* was destroyed, another would form in the same place. Having created an alternative urban geography where Black freedom was possible, even destroyed maroon villages continued to attract new escapees from slavery.[159]

In the Spanish Americas, Indigenous people similarly sought to use urban communities to achieve political autonomy but by co-opting rather than removing themselves from colonial urban institutions. *Indio* towns and *barrios* (neighborhoods), the successors of the early *reducciones*, often became strongholds of Indigenous community ties, cultural identity, and political authority. Their cabildos, created to enforce Spanish laws and the collection of labor tribute, helped to legitimize the power of elected Indigenous elites and to defend

153 "Freedom on the Move: A database of fugitives from American Slavery," https://freedomonthemove.org; Pargas, *Freedom Seekers*.

154 Helg, *Slave No More*, 43–63, 211–244.

155 Dantas, *Black Townsmen*, 1–10.

156 Schwartz, "The 'Mocambo'."

157 This plan is included in the documents related to the attack against the *quilombo* and apprehension of its members housed at the Arquivo Historico Ultramarino in Lisbon. It is discussed in Gomes and Reis, *Freedom by a Thread*.

158 Brown *Tacky's Revolt*, 108–128; Price, *First-Time*.

159 Price, *Maroon Societies*; Gomes and Reis, *Freedom by a Thread*; Dantas, "'For the Benefit of the Common Good'."

the interests of their communities.[160] Additionally, *Indios* and *Mestizos* (people of mixed Native and European descent) regularly engaged urban-based colonial courts, governors and viceroys, and Catholic authorities in the defense of their rights. Occasionally they succeeded in having imperial authorities arbitrate in their favor, against the interests of white settlers or colonial officers.[161]

Urban public spaces in Atlantic cities, such as streets, squares, and the porticos and yards of buildings, commonly staged displays of imperial and white power, from executions to political pageantry. In this manner, cities affirmed the dominant socio-racial hierarchy. But the discrete legal and political victories of Africans, Indigenous peoples, and their descendants were also visible within the city. In the Spanish Americas, those who secured urban residency and even *vecinidad* (citizenship) were notably excused from labor tribute obligations. In the Iberian Americas, those with a commercial or artisan license operated autonomously in urban economic spaces. And wherever Catholic religious associations (*confradías*) existed, those formed by Black or *Indio* members injected African and Indigenous American cultural traditions into urban festivities.[162]

For enslaved Africans and African descendants in the Americas, cities and towns were key to the pursuit of freedom through manumission and of their rights as freed people. By leveraging the relevance of their labor, Black men and women were sometimes able to secure wages with which to buy their freedom from enslavers. They relied on urban courts and notary offices to record their manumission and offer legal proof of their freedom when it was challenged or stolen. They also turned to courts and officials, both secular and ecclesiastical, to defend the sanctity of their marriages, the integrity of their families, and their right to property. Finally, through their Catholic religious associations or Protestant congregations, they occupied urban public spaces during festivals and ceremonies, claiming their right to the city itself.[163] Whether one thinks of New York, Baltimore, or New Orleans in North America, Salvador, Lima, or Buenos Aires in South America, and other sites in between, cities and towns were places where the enslavement of Black people and the racist dynamics it engendered were on full display. They were also places where the Black voices opposing that reality were particularly audible.

[160] Mumford, *Vertical Empire*, 57–73; Yannakakis, *The Art of Being In-Between*, 43–45; Murillo, *Urban Indians in a Silver City*, 87–116.

[161] Owensby, *Empire of Law*; Yannakakis, *The Art of Being In-Between*.

[162] Mangan, *Trading Roles*, 48–75; Graubart, *With Our Labor and Sweat*, 60–94; Murillo, *Urban Indians in a Silver City*, 117–158; Corbeil, *The Motions Beneath*, 162–184.

[163] Dantas, *Black Townsmen*, 97–126; White, *Voices of the Enslaved*, 48–95; Ball et al., *As If She Were Free*, 131–254; Hidalgo and Valerio, *Indigenous and Black Confraternities*, 63–180, 299–358.

By the late eighteenth century, moreover, Black, *Indio*, and *Mestizo* activists traveled from their cities in the Americas and Africa to European cities to request and demand white recognition of their rights and freedoms. Some succeeded in changing opinions, policies, and laws.[164] In 1772, for instance, James Somerset fled his enslaver in London and for that transgression he was threatened with sale to Jamaica and plantation slavery. With the help of an abolitionist network, the case for his freedom was presented to the Court of King's Bench, which decided in his favor. His victory set an important precedent for the legality of Black freedom.[165] In 1794, Jean-Baptiste Belley, a former slave and one of three deputies elected to represent Saint Domingue at the French Nation Convention in Paris, spoke passionately to that governing body in favor of abolition. His arguments influenced its decision to end slavery in the French empire.[166] These men's voices, heard in the capital of two European empires, amplified the plea thousands of others around the Atlantic made for the full freedom of those weighed down by white supremacy.

Enlightened Cities and the Rights of Some

By 1785, cities all around the Atlantic had witnessed, and fostered, political turmoil. London, Quito, New York, Caracas, Newcastle, and Charleston had been shaken by revolution, riots, or sustained protests that threatened to end the status quo of monarchical government. What is more, many of these ructions had clear connections to each other, with participants explicitly sharing ideas about rights and liberty across national or colonial borders. It was through these connections that Atlantic cities nurtured Atlantic freedoms. In an eighteenth-century context, such an exploration involved the close relationship between the city and the Enlightenment. A transoceanic network of thinkers, letters, ideas, and inquiry was ultimately what turned local protest into widespread revolution, and it relied on the city for its elaboration. In many Atlantic cities, however, the white male quest for "universal" rights unfolded against the backcloth of Black and Indigenous demands for freedom. The desire to confine the fruits of revolution to white beneficiaries thus circumscribed its extent in the Americas. The fear of Black urban radicalism was simply too great.

By the 1740s, Enlightenment networks had begun to encircle the ocean, flowing through transatlantic cities and transcending regional and local circuits of ideas and identities. Since towns formed the hubs of these networks, their intellectual institutions facilitated the sharing of knowledge among scientists,

164 Twinam, *Purchasing Whiteness*; Sparks, *The Two Princes*, 90–106; Semley, *To Be Free and French*, 1–68; Spieler, "Slave Voice and the Legal Archive"; Marquez, "Afflicted Slaves, Faithful Vassals."

165 Van Cleve, "Somerset's Case."

166 Levecq, *Black Cosmopolitans*, 75–159.

who developed new understandings of the natural world. At Philadelphia's American Philosophical Society, Charleston's Library Company, Newcastle upon Tyne's Thomlinson Library, Mexico City's Salons, or Paris's Academy of Sciences, urban men (and a few women) gathered to exchange learning and knowledge. In this way, urban centers around the Atlantic produced a globally connected, cosmopolitan, scientific community, who formulated their ideas as a result of evidence and discussion shared across thousands of miles. The development of the discipline of botany was the perfect example. Scientists and nurserymen in these urban spaces exchanged plant specimens, drawings, and new thinking about the classification of species to enrich knowledge of the natural world beyond Europe.[167]

This new botanical knowledge, primarily consisting of "curious" and "exotic" nature, was the Enlightenment's genteel aspect. Its urban political expression was less tranquil, however. By the 1760s, Enlightenment ideals underpinned an Atlantic-wide cry for liberty. In the wake of 1765's Stamp Tax, colonial American city dwellers gathered around their "liberty trees" and "liberty poles" as the Sons of Liberty. They marched through the streets in support of a radical solution to British taxation of Americans, expressing their ideals through direct action that often shaded into violence. Their cause acquired greater force through its interurban connections, nurtured through print and postal communication.[168]

In Britain's growing cities, middle-class tradesmen did not organize themselves as Sons of Liberty, but they nevertheless coalesced into identifiable protest movements. Among the most active were the citizen tradesmen of Newcastle upon Tyne, who mounted a vigorous campaign against the enclosure of the Town Moor in the 1770s. Although this was fundamentally a dispute about the privatization of common land, it became a vector for ideas about political liberty and representation. The case of the opposition crystallized in the pages of the *Newcastle Journal* and was then given additional force through correspondence with the future French revolutionary Jean-Paul Marat and the ideas of the famous radical English MP John Wilkes. Deploying these national and international discourses of liberty and rights, Newcastle's citizens halted the efforts of city elites to sell off the Moor and mounted their first successful challenge to an entrenched class of men who had represented the city as mayor and Member of Parliament for centuries.[169]

These were not simply popular protests, however. What made them revolutionary in North America was their co-option by elites who had now also

[167] Easterby-Smith, *Cultivating Commerce*, 147–173; Chaplin, *First Scientific American*; Parsons, *Not-So-New World*, 125–151.

[168] Nash, *Urban Crucible*; Parkinson, *Thirteen Clocks*.

[169] Wilson, *Sense of the People*, 345–358; Hammersley, "Jean Paul Marat's 'The Chains of Slavery'."

become disillusioned with the limits that imperial rule placed on their liberty. Working across class lines, American patriots used urban-based communication networks to create intellectual connections among like-minded people. Networks spanned the Atlantic in a "republic of letters" that joined members of America's Continental Congress in Philadelphia with Jean-Jacques Rousseau. They drew Thomas Paine from the sleepy English town of Lewes to Philadelphia, a hub of the American Revolution. There, he found printers willing to disseminate his pamphlet *Common Sense*, a work that then was carried to Boston, New York, and Charleston. The cities of the so-called thirteen colonies had become linchpins in the formation of a revolutionary movement. This status made them valuable prizes in the war between the British and their former colonial subjects; King George's troops occupied New York for almost the whole conflict, while Newport (Rhode Island), Philadelphia, Charleston, and Savannah all suffered the same fate for periods of it.[170]

Once they had claimed victory over the British, elite Americans such as Benjamin Franklin, John Adams, and Thomas Jefferson traveled to Paris, where they burnished their reputations as Republicans. Together, these gentlemen revolutionaries connected cities in opposition to imperial and monarchical power. Though many of these cities were originally designed as manifestations of that power, transatlantic hubs such as Boston and Philadelphia had now nurtured these Republican ideologues, thus producing some of the monarchy's chief adversaries.

As the first revolutionaries to cast off imperial power, Americans played a role in encouraging republicanism around the Atlantic. Cities were once again the chief vehicle of these connections. By the 1800s, Philadelphia was a place of resort for Iberian American revolutionaries. Exiled there in the 1790s after an attempted uprising against the Spanish crown, Colombian Manuel Torres was a prominent member of this community. His home rapidly became a North American hub for networks of anti-imperial agitators. With Americans increasingly viewing themselves as part of a hemispheric uprising against colonialism, urban elites happily entertained visitors like Antônio Gonçalves da Cruz, a resident of Pernambuco in northeastern Brazil looking for funds to support the uprising of his state against Portuguese imperial rule. Da Cruz toured the biggest cities of the American northeast, publicizing his cause in the local press as he went and bending the ear of the most important politicians, who seemed eager to assist his noble quest against imperialism.[171]

---

[170] Parkinson, *Thirteen Clocks*; Gray, *Tom's Paine's Iron Bridge*; Johnson, *Occupied America*.

[171] Fitz, *Our Sister Republics*, 48–51.

Cities in the Iberian world did not possess the complex networks of printed communication necessary to spread Enlightenment ideas with as much efficiency as they had in British America. Still, men like da Cruz were just as up to date with Enlightenment philosophies of government as their northern compatriots. Spanish translations of documents such as the Declaration of Independence made their way to urban centers thanks to American merchants. With the unpopularity of the Bourbon reforms among creole elites, and then the toppling of the Iberian monarchies in the wake of Napoleon's 1808 invasion of the metropole, came the moment for these Enlightenment ideas of rights to be put to work in South America.[172]

Led by Bolivar's bid for Venezuelan independence, these movements were every bit as violent and drawn out as the Atlantic revolutions that had preceded them. They were also just as reliant on urban centers for their success. Bolivar attempted to take power by seizing strategic cities including, of course, the capital of Caracas. At the opposite end of the continent the power struggle was also urban as warring factions fought over Montevideo and Buenos Aires for control of the Rio de la Plata region. Yet, while cities were revolutionary strongholds, their hinterlands often remained bastions of loyalism.[173]

While rural resistance temporarily checked some Iberian revolutionary movements, the power and populousness of Black and Indigenous people would act as a permanent brake on radicalism. Early on, Iberian elites rejected the French experience of revolution, their fear of it only intensifying with the Haitian Revolution in 1791. To these elites, it seemed as if their worst fears were materializing when a Black and *pardo* revolt unfolded in Coro, a town in Venezuela. Its leaders, Jose Leonardo Chirino and Jose Caridad Gonzalez, were free Black men who had traveled around the Caribbean and learned of the Haitian Revolution's success. Soon, Black Haitians were banned altogether from entering the Iberian Americas.[174]

White North Americans went to no such lengths, but not because they were in favor of extending the privilege of liberty to the enslaved and free Black people in their midst. As well as being a destination for would-be Iberian revolutionaries, Philadelphia had in the 1790s also become a refuge for French and Haitian exiles seeking to *escape* revolution. As the young U.S. Republic forged ever stronger bonds with revolutionary France, close ties to both the metropole and its Caribbean possessions proliferated. Thousands of French citizens settled in Philadelphia, opening businesses and facilitating the trade in flour, sugar, and

---

172 Uribe-Uran, "The Birth of a Public Sphere"; McFarlane, "Rebellions in Late Colonial Spanish America."

173 Kinsbruner, *Independence in Spanish America.*

174 Scott, *Common Wind*, 177–179; Walker, *Smoldering Ashes*, 184–220.

coffee that bound the city's merchant community to Saint Domingue's planters. When the Haitian Revolution threatened the wealth and power of these planters, Philadelphia's newspapers brought a steady stream of updates on the state of the revolt, while the city's wharves welcomed an influx of white French refugees and their enslaved African people. In 1793, these Haitian transplants also brought yellow fever with them. The subsequent outbreak killed some 10 percent of Philadelphia's inhabitants, making it the most fatal epidemic in American history.[175] These close ties meant that white Americans knew and feared the consequences of Black access to revolutionary ideals.

It was thus in cities that Americans sought, through legal and extralegal means, to prevent Black access to the liberties that they themselves enjoyed. The intensity of white efforts to block Black and Indigenous access to revolutionary discourses of rights was strongly connected to the size of a city's non-white population. In Boston, which had a substantial white majority, enslaved and free Blacks such as Prince Hall had begun to argue for their human rights. Although Pennsylvania would pass an emancipation law in 1780, this did not prevent Philadelphia from becoming the focus of a growing conflict between the young nation's white governing classes and its diverse population. The city grew quickly as a center of Black life, with free African Americans establishing their own churches, schools, and businesses. Black people were attracted by the economic opportunities of a growing city as well as the presence of a welcoming community, and these money-making possibilities also drew in an array of poor white laborers. Although such people were essential workers, elites often viewed them as a criminal element in need of better regulation. Thus, early Republic Philadelphia was also a place where African Americans faced increasing aggression from white city dwellers and where one of America's earliest penitentiaries was opened in 1818.[176]

Still, the force of white aggression was weak compared to those cities in which the Black population was larger still. In Charleston, South Carolina, enslaved people suffered at the hands of ruling whites who were terrified of a Black uprising. Successful free Black Charlestonians like Thomas Jeremiah and Denmark Vesey were murdered as suspected leaders of slave revolts, despite the highly questionable nature of the accusations against them. Separated by forty-seven years, Jeremiah's 1775 death and Vesey's 1822 demise bookended an era in which white Charlestonians diligently worked to circumscribe the freedoms of the free and enslaved Africans in their midst. Their deaths were therefore only the most spectacular aspect of repression.

---

175 Dun, *Dangerous Neighbors*, 1–26.

176 Sesay, "Dialectic of Representation"; Nash, *Forging Freedom*; Manion, *Liberty's Prisoners*.

Much more mundane was the torrent of legislation that came from Charleston's revivified urban government. Seeking to limit Black urban economic activity and associated mobility around the city and the region, city rulers created a host of regulations as part of their new corporate government. Adhering to the sentiment that such people needed policing and controlling, Blacks found themselves subject to curfews preventing them from leaving their owners' homes after dark and forced at nightfall to scuttle back to their domestic imprisonment at the ringing of a bell.[177]

The closer one got to Haiti, the more conservative and brutal the white rulers became in their efforts to deny the liberties they enjoyed to urban Africans. New Orleans' large Black population felt the web of regulation and repression closing more tightly around them, first as refugees from Haiti arrived with news of the revolt and then as the city was absorbed in the brutal slave regimes of the United States' Deep South cotton and sugar economy. As the city became the marketplace of the internal slave trade, efforts to confine and punish free and enslaved Black residents intensified.[178]

At the very end of this spectrum of intensifying repression lay the Cuban urban experience. The Enlightenment discourse of rights could not reach the island's flourishing towns of Havana and Santiago. There, elites were deeply committed to building a sugar economy founded on the importation of hundreds of thousands of Africans, laboring in slavery in the shadow of the free Black republic of Haiti. Cuba's governor, Francisco Arango, saw to it that loyalty to Spain and political stability would buttress a brutally repressive slave society. Such measures could not stop Havana's large and long-standing Black residents from acting on the revolutionary spirit brought to the city by immigrants from the United States and Haiti and nurtured by leaders like Jose Antonio Aponte, who led an 1812 uprising. The consequences for Aponte of the revolt – which was designed to progress from the city outward to the countryside – were a brutal death and the display of his head on a spike in Havana as a reminder for all Afro-Cubans of the costs of claiming liberty.[179]

Thus it was that, by the 1830s, Atlantic cities had become both the seedbed of revolution and the generators of revolutionary backlash. That backlash was also felt in British cities, where the discourse of liberty and rights imported from the French Revolution emboldened working men to organize and march against England's ruling aristocracy. The expressions of this opposition – such as the London Corresponding Society and the urban protests in support of electoral

[177] Harris, *Hanging of Thomas Jeremiah*; Johnson, "Denmark Vesey and His Co-conspirators"; Hart, *Trading Spaces*, 177–189; Haney, "Understanding Antebellum Charleston's Backlots through Light and Sound."

[178] Johnson, *Slavery's Metropolis*; Johnson, *Wicked Flesh*.

[179] Ferrer, *Cuba*, 41–78.

reform – were effectively suppressed with military and political might. Nevertheless, the determination of white urban elites to hold on to their power was strongest in those cities where their freedom stood in starkest contrast to Black and Indigenous unfreedoms. Around the Atlantic, the city had become both the generator of revolution and the originator of its limits. And the more radical the promise, the more brutal the backlash.

Conclusion

Because they fostered bids for liberty and rights among their white, Black, and Indigenous inhabitants, Atlantic cities embodied the power struggles that the Atlantic system had created. Out of these struggles came glimpses of a victory for the subjugated majority. For those formerly enslaved people who joined the nation-founding expeditions to Sierra Leone and Liberia, their capitals, Freetown and Monrovia, represented a new type of Atlantic city built on the foundations of commerce, Christianity, and community (Figure 11). Attracting immigrants from Europe and the Americas, the towns acted as beacons for the anti-slavery cause. In many ways in competition with each other, they reflected the contrasting North American and British approaches to abolitionism and a longer-standing argument within the Anglo-Atlantic. Nevertheless, they were also the foundation of a new role for West African cities in this Atlantic world as they promoted "freedom" and not enslavement.[180]

While Monrovia and Freetown were integral to the growing Atlantic anti-slavery movement, Luanda and Benguela remained hubs of the slave trade. The growth of abolitionism ushered in a new relationship for cities with Black freedom and unfreedom – one in which cities on the same continent could grow as important bastions of anti-slavery while others flourished equally on slavery. Likewise, Philadelphia, Boston, and New York became home to quickly growing free Black populations by the early nineteenth century. Further south in the young United States, however, other cities were growing just as fast on the foundations of enslaving ever more Black people. Washington DC, Richmond (Virginia), and New Orleans enjoyed new notoriety as centers of an internal slave trade that moved people from the "old" south to the "new" one, where they were forced to work on brutal cotton plantations.[181]

Ultimately, it would be the inequality and slavery characterizing these cities that pointed the way to the future as an Atlantic world transitioned to a globalized one. As scholars such as Saskia Sassen have highlighted, the global city thrives on inequality between the owners of global capital and the workers

[180] Everill, *Abolition and Empire*; Scanlan, *Freedom's Debtors*.

[181] Ferreira, *Cross-Cultural Exchange*; Deyle, *Carry Me Back*; Johnson, *Soul by Soul*.

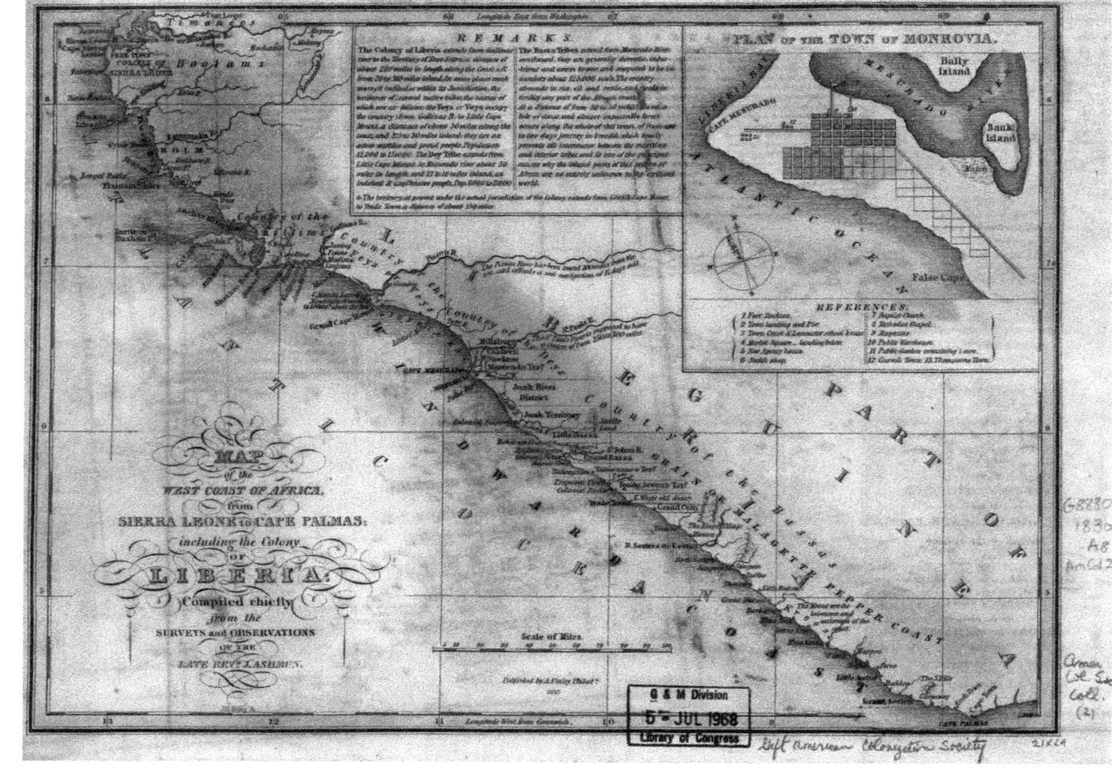

Figure 11 Map of Liberia with plan of the town of Monrovia (1830).

J. Ashmun, J. H. Young, and A. Finley, “Map of the West Coast of Africa from Sierra Leone to Cape Palmas, including the colony of Liberia” (Philadelphia, PA: A. Finley, 1830), Map. Library of Congress, Geography and Map Division. www.loc.gov/item/96680499/.

who service them.[182] The foundations of urban systems that thrive on the denial of rights to some by others who grow rich from long-distance networks are rooted in the political and economic developments fostered by the creation of Atlantic urbanism.

5 Conclusion

In his book about Portuguese Angola, the historian Roquinaldo Ferreira recounts the drama surrounding an 1824 sedition scare in the city of Benguela. A group of wealthy merchants were arrested, accused of planning Benguela's secession from Angola and annexation to the nation of Brazil, which had achieved its independence from Portugal in 1822. The alleged leader of the movement was Francisco Ferreira Gomes, a Black man born in Rio de Janeiro. Aside from highlighting the transatlantic commercial connections between Brazil and Angola, this episode recalls European imperial anxieties over the exchange of political ideals and ambitions promoted by Atlantic cities. Gomes's African ancestry also raised the specter of Haiti and a race war, adding to the fears of white Portuguese imperial agents. Surrounded by Black militia troops and in a minority, white Benguela residents were quite aware of their vulnerability. In the end, the suspected sedition was never proven to be more than a rumor, which had gained traction because of the city of Benguela's past struggles for political and economic autonomy in Angola.[183]

The persecution of an unproven sedition in the city of Benguela was just one of many dramatic events unfolding in and between Atlantic cities in the early nineteenth century. Just a year earlier, in 1823, patriotic troops marched victoriously through Salvador, Brazil, after a year-long siege of the city forced the surrender of loyalist Portuguese forces.[184] Two years prior, Mexico City was the stage of the triumphant entrance of the royalist officer turned patriotic leader Agustín de Iturbide and the multiple civic rituals celebrating Mexican independence that followed.[185] Across the ocean in 1819, peaceful working-class protestors demanding parliamentary reform in the industrializing town of Manchester were met with a brutal cavalry charge that killed some and injured hundreds in a matter of minutes.[186] The Peterloo Massacre added to the turbulence of Britain's Regency era, during which British forces had captured and set fire to the government buildings of another city symbolic of Atlantic political reformist currents, Washington DC (Figure 12).[187] Although the imperial Atlantic was now giving way to an oceanic world of nation-states, and an

182 Sassen, "The Global City." 183 Ferreira, *Cross-Cultural Exchange*, 203–241.
184 Kraay, *Bahia's Independence*, 3–5.
185 Hensel, "La Coronación de Agustín I," 1357–1361. 186 Poole, *Peterloo*.
187 Eustace, *1812*, 168–210.

Figure 12 The capture of Washington by British forces, August 24, 1814 (1815).

Washington. A representation of the capture of the city of Washington, by the British forces under the command of Major Genl. Ross and Rear Adml. Sir I. Cockburn, August 24th, wherein are shown, the fort and the flotilla. (England: Publish'd by I. Ryland 83, Cannon Street, 1815). Photograph. Library of Congress, Prints & Photographs Division. www.loc.gov/item/2012645366/.

increasingly globally connected one at that, cities remained the motors of political change and the focus of dissent.

For nearly four centuries, cities, towns, and even villages around the Atlantic basin had played this role. Sometimes helping to foment discord and conflict, at other times facilitating consensus and unity, but at all times enabling those exchanges, cities were key to shaping the early modern Atlantic. Politically, economically, culturally, and socially, cities of many sizes and characters had grown to become the engines of Atlantic, and increasingly global, processes of change.

In this way, the centuries between 1500 and 1850 were a founding era of global urban life. As Carl Nightingale has argued, "earthopolis" – our global urban planet – began to take shape in the early modern period. In the era when distinct oceanic systems emerged and then began to coalesce into one world ocean, cities emerged as the keystones in these networks.[188] Not simply ports, or symbols of imperial power, transatlantic, regional, and local cities played dual roles as drivers of connection and drivers of conflict. What is more, this is a role that we can identify in the majority of early modern Atlantic cities – something that made them foundational to urban dynamics that would become widely significant in a more globalized, more urbanized future.

[188] Games, "Atlantic History"; Dantas and Hart, "Digging Down into the Global Urban Past."

We hope that the reader will profit from the insights that can be gleaned from this analysis of how it was that cities became the centers of an imperial system's core networks, ideologies, tensions, and inequalities. Here, we have explained how cities' foundational role came to be and why the city as an entity was so crucial. Cities were viewed by Europeans as a vehicle of imperialism. They could be (and were) very effective in this capacity. Yet, right from their establishment, inhabitants challenged the limits of imperial control. As the Atlantic imperial city grew in size and importance through the seventeenth and eighteenth centuries, the negotiation between the forces of imperial control and local constituencies of urban citizens came to rest at the core of urban society, economy, and politics. The tension between the local and the imperial reached a crescendo in the age of the Atlantic Revolution, when cities became origin points for colonial uprisings. The long-standing struggles within cities between white ruling men and a majority Black and Indigenous citizenry would ultimately limit the extent of these uprisings, however. Thus was a dynamic established in which the city would be a vehicle of cosmopolitanism, capitalism, and inequality. It was a dynamic that would only grow more prevalent on a global scale in the nineteenth century.

Only some of the cities discussed in this Element would grow to become the global metropolises that form the hubs of our world systems today. Readers will no doubt have recognized these places: New York, London, Paris, Mexico City, Monrovia, and Rio de Janeiro. They may also question why we also chose to incorporate some cities that seem to be little more than villages or which faded from importance as the 1800s progressed: Newport (Rhode Island), Saint Louis (Senegal), Ouro Preto (Minas Gerais), or Bridgetown (Barbados). If we are to understand how cities fostered the cosmopolitanism, capitalism, and inequality that are characteristic of the contemporary global metropolis, we need to trace their emergence in the widest possible array of urban contexts. Some of these contexts represent roads not taken if viewed only in a single place. Nevertheless, the story becomes much more significant when we pull back to regard the city on the much broader canvas that was the early modern Atlantic world.

Bibliography

Abu-Lughod, J. *Before European Hegemony: The World System A.D. 1250–1350*. New York: Oxford University Press, 1989.

Altman, I. "Key to the Indies: Port Towns in the Spanish Caribbean, 1493–1550." *The Americas* 74, no. 1 (2017), 5–26.

Altman, I. *Life and Society in the Early Spanish Caribbean: The Greater Antilles, 1493–1550*. Baton Rouge: Louisiana State University Press, 2021.

Anastasia, C. M. J. *Vassalos Rebeldes: violência coletiva nas Minas na primeira metade do Século XVIII*. Belo Horizonte: Editora C/Arte, 1998.

Andrade, A. E. *A invenção das Minas Gerais: empresas, descobrimentos e entradas nos sertões do ouro da América Portuguesa*. Belo Horizonte: Autêntica Editora, 2008.

Arnold, T. S. "Central Europe and the Portuguese, Spanish and French Atlantic, Fifteenth to Nineteenth Centuries." *European Review* 26, no. 3 (2018), 421–429.

Asenjo-González, M., García, D. A., and Perrone, S. "Town and Country: Connecting Late Medieval Castilian Urban Experience with Sixteenth-Century Colonization of the Americas." *Bulletin for Spanish and Portuguese Historical Studies* 44 (2019), 7–32. https://doi.org/10.26431/0739-182X.1326.

Badillo, J. S. "Guadalupe: Caribe o Taína? La Isla de Guadalupe Y Su Cuestionable Identidad Caribe en la Época Pre-Colombina: Una Revisión Etnohistórica Y Arqueológica Preliminar." *Caribbean Studies* 35, no. 1 (2007), 35–85.

Bailey, G. A. *Art of Colonial Latin America*. London: Phaidon Press, 2005.

Bakewell, P. *Silver Mining and Society in Colonial Mexico, Zacatecas 1546–1700*. Cambridge: Cambridge University Press, 1971.

Ball, E. L., Seijas, T., and Snyder, T. L. *As If She Were Free: A Collective Biography of Women and Emancipation in the Americas*. Cambridge: Cambridge University Press, 2020.

Barrett, C. J. "Origins of the French Bastides." *Journal of Urban History* 44, no. 3 (2018), 421–456.

Baumanova, M., Smejda, L., and Rüther, H. "Pre-colonial Origins of Urban Spaces in the West African Sahel: Street Networks, Trade, and Spatial Plurality." *Journal of Urban History* 45, no. 3 (2019), 500–519.

Bennett, H. L. *African Kings and Black Slaves: Sovereignty and Dispossession in the Early Modern Atlantic*. Philadelphia: University of Pennsylvania Press, 2018.

Bense, J. A. "Introduction: Presidios of the North American Spanish Borderlands." *Historical Archaeology* 38, no. 3 (2004), 1–5.

Bermejo, S. M. "Lisbon, New Rome and Emporium: Comparing an Early Modern Imperial Capital, 1550–1750." *Urban History* 44, no. 4 (2017), 604–621.

Bicalho, M. F. *A cidade e o império: O Rio de Janeiro no século XVIII*. Rio de Janeiro: Civilização Brasileira, 2003.

Boehm, L. K. and Corey, S. H. *America's Urban History*. New York: Routledge, 2015.

Boone, J. and Benco, N. "Islamic Settlement in North Africa and the Iberian Peninsula." *Annual Review of Anthropology* 28 (1999), 51–71.

Boone, M. "Medieval Europe." In *The Oxford Handbook of Cities in World History*, edited by P. Clark, 222–239. New York: Oxford University Press, 2013.

Brown, V. *Tacky's Revolt: The Story of an Atlantic Slave War*. Cambridge, MA: Harvard University Press, 2020.

Burkholder, M. and Johnson, L. *Colonial Latin America*. Oxford: Oxford University Press, 2001.

Burnard, T. "Slaves and Slavery in Kingston, 1770–1815." *International Review of Social History* 65, no. S28 (2020), 39–65.

Burnard, T. and Hart, E. "Kingston, Jamaica, and Charleston, South Carolina: A New Look at Comparative Urbanization in Plantation Colonial British America." *Journal of Urban History* 39, no. 2 (2013), 214–234.

Calabi, D. "Early Modern Port Cities: Harbouring Ships and Residential Settlement." In *Waterfronts Revisited: European Ports in a Historic and Global Perspective*, edited by H. Porfyriou and M. Sepe, 19–25. New York: Routledge, 2016.

Candiani, V. S. *Dreaming of Dry Land: Environmental Transformation in Colonial Mexico City*. Stanford, CA: Stanford University Press, 2014.

Candido, M. *An African Slaving Port and the Atlantic World: Benguela and Its hinterland*. Cambridge: Cambridge University Press, 2015.

Caracausi, A. and Jeggle, C. *Commercial Networks and European Cities, 1400–1800*. London: Taylor & Francis, 2015.

Carretta, V. *Unchained Voices: An Anthology of Black Authors in the English-Speaking World of the Eighteenth Century*. Lexington: University Press of Kentucky, 1996.

Chakravarti, A. "Invisible Cities: Natural and Social Space in Colonial Brazil." In *Cities and the Circulation of Culture in the Atlantic World*, edited by L. von Morzé, 13–36. New York: Palgrave, 2017.

Chaplin, J. "The Atlantic Ocean and Its Contemporary Meanings, 1492–1808." In *Atlantic History: A Critical Appraisal*, edited by J. P. Greene and P. D. Morgan, 35–54. New York: Oxford University Press, 2008.

Chaplin, J. *The First Scientific American: Benjamin Franklin and the Pursuit of Genius*. New York: Basic Books, 2007.

Christie, J. J. "The Inka Capital Cusco as the Model of an Imperial Cultural Landscape." In *Political Landscapes of Capital Cities*, edited by J. J. Christie, J. Bogdanovic, and E. Guzmán, 213–247. Boulder: University Press of Colorado, 2016.

Chrysostomo, M. I. J. "L'urbanisation des marges de la colonie: l'aldeamento de Guarulhos et la naissance des paroisses, *vilas* et *cidades* de la région fluviale de Campos dos Goytacazes." In *Les Fondations de Villes sur les Litoraux Américains: Brèsil et États-Unis, XVI*[e]*–XIX*[e] *siècles*, edited by L. Vidal and B. Ruymbeke, 85–116. Reines: Les Perseides, 2021.

Chuku, G., ed. *The Igbo Intellectual Tradition: Creative Conflict in African and African Diasporic Thought*. New York: Palgrave Macmillan, 2016.

Clark, P. *British Clubs and Societies, 1580–1800: The Origins of an Associational World*. Oxford: Oxford University Press, 2000.

Clark, P. *European Cities and Towns: 400–2000*. New York: Oxford University Press, 2009.

Clark, P., ed. *The Oxford Handbook of Cities in World History*. Oxford: Oxford University Press, 2013.

Clendinnen, I. *Ambivalent Conquests: Maya and Spanish in the Yucatan, 1517–1570*. Cambridge: Cambridge University Press, 1987.

Connah, G. "Contained Communities in Tropical Africa." In *City Walls: The Urban Enceinte in Global Perspective*, edited by J. Tracy, 19–45. Cambridge: Cambridge University Press, 2000.

Cope, R. D. *The Limits of Racial Domination: Plebeian Society in Colonial Mexico City, 1660–1720*. Madison: University of Wisconsin Press, 1994.

Coquery-Vidrovitch, C. *The History of African Cities South of the Sahara*. Princeton, NJ: Markus Wiener Publications, 2005.

Corbeil, L. *The Motions Beneath: Indigenous Migrants on the Urban Frontiers of New Spain*. Phoenix: University of Arizona Press, 2018.

Cortés, H. *Five Letter, 1519–1526*, translated by F. B. Morris. New York: W. W. Norton & Company, 1991.

Cromwell, J. *The Smugglers' World: Illicit Trade and Atlantic Communities in Eighteenth-Century Venezuela*. Chapel Hill: University of North Carolina Press, 2018.

Crosby, A. *The Columbian Exchange: Biological and Cultural Consequences of 1492*. Westport, CT: Greenwood, 1972.

Cruz, G. *Let There Be Towns: Spanish Municipal Origins in the American Southwest, 1610–1818*. College Station: Texas A&M University Press, 1988.

Curcio-Nagy, L. A. *The Great Festivals of Colonial Mexico City: Performing Power and Identity*. Albuquerque: University of New Mexico Press, 2004.

Dantas, M. *Black Townsmen: Urban Slavery and Freedom in the Eighteenth-Century Americas*. New York: Palgrave, 2008.

Dantas, M. "'For the Benefit of the Common Good': Regiments of Cacadores do Mato in Minas Gerais, Brazil." *Journal of Colonialism and Colonial History* 5, no. 2 (2004). https://doi.org/10.1353/cch.2004.0046.

Dantas, M. "Une autre lecture des fondations urbaines: les confréries noires et la vie civique dans les villes minières du Brésil Colonial." In *Les fondations de villes sur les littoraux américains: Brésil et États-Unis, XVIe–XIXe siècles*, edited by L. Vidal and B. V. Ruymbeke, 267–283. Reines: Les Perséides, 2021.

Dantas, M. and Hart, E. "Digging Down into the Global Urban Past." *Urban History* 48, no. 3 (2021), 424–434.

Davenport, B. and Golden, C. "Landscapes, Lordships, and Sovereignty in Mesoamerica." In *Political Strategies in Pre-Columbian Mesoamerica*, edited by S. Kurnick and J. Barron, 181–216. Boulder: University Press of Colorado, 2016.

Deagan, K. "Strategies of Adjustment: Spanish Defense of the Circum-Caribbean Colonies, 1493–1600." In *First Forts: Essays on the Archaeology of Proto-colonial Fortifications*, edited by E. Klingelhofer, 17–39. Leiden: Brill, 2012.

Deagan, K. and Cruxent, J. M. *Columbus's Outpost among the Taínos: Spain and America at La Isabela, 1493–1498*. New Haven, CT: Yale University Press, 2002.

Dean, C. *Inka Bodies and the Body of Christ: Corpus Christi in Colonial Cuzco, Peru*. Durham, NC: Duke University Press, 1999.

DeCorse, C. R. *An Archaeology of Elmina: Africans and Europeans on the Gold Coast, 1400–1900*. Washington, DC: Smithsonian Institution Press, 2001.

Deyle, S. *Carry Me Back: The Domestic Slave Trade in American Life*. New York: Oxford University Press, 2006.

Díaz, R. A. *Esclavitud, región y ciudad: el sistema esclavista urbano-regional en Santafé de Bogotá, 1700–1750*. Bogotá: Centro Editorial Javeriano, 2001.

Dun, A. *Dangerous Neighbors: Making the Haitian Revolution in Early America*. Philadelphia: University of Pennsylvania Press, 2016.

Dunn, R. E. *The Adventures of Ibn Battuta: A Muslim Traveler of the Fourteenth Century*. Berkeley: University of California Press, 2005.

Dym, J. *From Sovereign Villages to National States: City, State, and Federation in Central America, 1759–1839*. Albuquerque: University of New Mexico Press, 2006.

Easterby-Smith, S. *Cultivating Commerce: Cultures of Botany in Britain and France, 1760–1815*. Cambridge: Cambridge University Press, 2018.

Elbl, M. "Portuguese Urban Fortifications in Morocco: Borrowing, Adaptations, and Innovation along a Military Frontier." In *City Walls: The Urban Enceinte in Global Perspective*, edited by J. D. Tracy, 349–385. New York: Cambridge University Press, 2000.

Enthoven, V. "'That Abominable Nest of Pirates': St. Eustatius and the North Americans, 1680—1780." *Early American Studies* 10, no. 2 (2012), 239–301.

Equiano, O. *The Interesting Narrative and Other Writings*. London: Penguin, 2003.

Eustace, N. *1812: War and the Passions of Patriotism*. Philadelphia: University of Pennsylvania Press, 2012.

Everill, B. *Abolition and Empire in Sierra Leone and Liberia*. New York: Palgrave Macmillan, 2013.

Fair, J. E., Harbsmeier, M., and Whitehead, N. L., eds. *Hans Staden's True History: An Account of Cannibal Captivity in Brazil*. Durham, NC: Duke University Press, 2008.

Ferdinand, C. Y. *Benjamin Collins and the Provincial Newspaper Trade in the Eighteenth Century*. Oxford: Oxford University Press, 1997.

Ferreira, R. *Cross-Cultural Exchange in the Atlantic World: Angola and Brazil during the Era of the Slave Trade*. New York: Cambridge University Press, 2012.

Ferrer, A. *Cuba: An American History*. London: Simon & Schuster, 2021.

Finger, S. *The Contagious City: The Politics of Public Health in early Philadelphia*. Ithaca, NY: Cornell University Press, 2012.

Fitz, C. *Our Sister Republics: The United States in an Age of Revolution*. New York: W. W. Norton & Co., 2016.

Flickema, T. "The Siege of Cuzco." *Revista de Historia de América* 92 (1981), 17–47.

Fonseca, C. D. *Arraiais e Vilas D'el Rei: Espaço e Poder nas Minas Setecentistas*. Belo Horizonte: Editora UFMG, 2011.

Freund, B. *The African City: A History*. Cambridge: Cambridge University Press, 2007.

Fuentes, M. *Dispossessed Lives: Enslaved Women, Violence and the Archive*. Philadelphia: University of Pennsylvania Press, 2016.

Games, A. "Atlantic History: Definitions, Challenges, and Opportunities." *The American Historical Review* 111, no. 3 (2006), 741–757.

Garrido, F. "Rethinking Imperial Infrastructure: A Bottom-Up Perspective on the Inca Road." *Journal of Anthropology and Archaeology* 43 (2016), 94–109.

Gitlin, J. *The Bourgeois Frontier: French Towns, French Traders, and American Expansion*. New Haven, CT: Yale University Press, 2009.

Gomes, F. S. and Reis, J. J. *Freedom by a Thread: The History of Quilombos in Brazil*. La Vergne: Diasporic Africa Press, 2017.

Gouvêa, M. F. "Redes de poder na América portuguesa: O caso dos homens bons do Rio de Janeiro, 1790–1822." *Revista Brasileira de História* 18, no. 36 (1998), 297–330.

Graubart, K. B. *With Our Labor and Sweat: Indigenous Women and the Formation of Colonial Society in Peru, 1550–1700*. Stanford, CA: Stanford University Press, 2007.

Gray, E. *Tom Paine's Iron Bridge: Building a United States*. New York: W. W. Norton & Co., 2016.

Griffeth, R. "The Hausa City-States from 1450–1804." In *A Comparative Study of Thirty City-State Cultures: An Investigation*, edited by M. H. Hansen, 483–506. Copenhagen: The Royal Danish Academy of Sciences and Letters, 2000.

Gutiérrez, R. A. *When Jesus Came, the Corn Mothers Went Away: Marriage, Sexuality, and Power in New Mexico, 1500–1846*. Stanford, CA: Stanford University Press, 1991.

Hagen, C. and Morris, C. *The Cities of the Ancient Andes*. London: Thames and Hudson, 1998.

Hamalainen, P. *The Comanche Empire*. New Haven, CT: Yale University Press, 2008.

Hammersley, R. "Jean-Paul Marat's 'The Chains of Slavery' in Britain and France, 1774–1833." *The Historical Journal* 48, no. 3 (2005), 641–660.

Hancock, D. *Citizens of the World: London Merchants and the Integration of the British Atlantic Community, 1735–1785*. Cambridge: Cambridge University Press, 2013.

Haney, G. "Understanding Antebellum Charleston's Backlots through Light, Sound, and Action." In *Slavery in the City: Architecture and Landscapes of Urban Slavery in North America*, edited by C. Ellis and R. Ginsburg, 87–105. Charlottesville: University of Virginia Press, 2017.

Hanna, M. G. *Pirate Nests and the Rise of the British Empire, 1570–1740*. Chapel Hill: University of North Carolina Press, 2015.

Harriot, T. *A Brief and True Report of the New Found Land of Virginia*. London, 1588.

Harris, J. W. *The Hanging of Thomas Jeremiah: A Free Black Man's Encounter with Liberty*. New Haven, CT: Yale University Press, 2009.

Hart, E. *Trading Spaces: The Colonial Marketplace and the Foundations of American Capitalism*. Chicago, IL: University of Chicago Press, 2019.

Haslip-Viera, G. "The Underclass." In *Cities and Societies in Colonial Latin America*, edited by L. S. Hoberman and S. M. Socolow, 285–312. Albuquerque: University of New Mexico Press, 1986.

Hausberger, B. and Hough-Snee, D. Z. "Precious Metals in the Americas at the Beginning of the Global Economy." In *Iberian Empires and the Roots of Globalization*, edited by I. del Valle, A. More, and R. O'Toole, 23–39. Nashville, TN: Vanderbilt University Press, 2020.

Havard, G. *Empire et métissages: Indiens et Français dans le Pays d'en Haut, 1660–1715*. Paris: Septentrion, 2003.

Heckscher, E. *Mercantilism*. New York: Routledge, 1994.

Helg, A. *Slave No More: Self-Liberation before Abolitionism in the Americas*. Chapel Hill: University of North Carolina Press, 2019.

Hensel, Silke. "La Coronación de Agustín I. Un Ritual Ambiguo en la Transición Mexicana del Antiguo Régimen a la independencia." *Historia Mexicana* 61, no. 4 (244) (2012), 1349–1411.

Herzog, T. *Defining Nations: Immigrants and Citizens in Early Modern Spain and Spanish America*. New Haven, CT: Yale University Press, 2008.

Herzog, T. "Indigenous *Reducciones* and Spanish Resettlement: Placing Colonial and European History in Dialogue." *Ler História* 72 (2018), 9–30.

Heyden, D. "From Teotihuacan to Tenochtitlan: City Planning, Caves, and Streams of Red and Blue Waters." In *Mesoamerica's Classic Heritage: From Teotihuacan to the Aztecs*, edited by D. Carrasco, L. Jones, and S. Sessions, 165–184. Boulder: University Press of Colorado, 2000.

Heywood, L. M. *Njinga of Angola: Africa's Warrior Queen*. Cambridge, MA: Harvard University Press, 2017.

Hidalgo, J. J. and Valerio, M., eds. *Indigenous and Black Confraternities in Colonial Latin America*. Amsterdam: Amsterdam University Press, 2022.

Hidalgo, J. and Valerio, M. "Negotiating Status through Confraternal Practices." In *Indigenous and Black Confraternities in Colonial Latin America: Negotiating Status through Religious Practices*, edited by J. Hidalgo and M. Valerio, 9–36. Amsterdam: Amsterdam University Press, 2022.

Hobsbawm, E. *The Age of Revolution: Europe, 1789–1848*. London: Knopf Doubleday, 1996.

Hopkins, K. Y. "A New Landscape: Changing Iroquois Settlement Patterns, Subsistence Strategies, and Environmental Use, 1630–1783." PhD dissertation, University of California, Davis, 2010.

Hoppit, J. "Patterns of Parliamentary Legislation, 1660–1800." *The Historical Journal* 39, no. 1 (1996), 109–131.

Horn, J. *A Brave and Cunning Prince: The Great Chief Opechancanough and the War for America*. New York: Basic Books, 2021.

Hornsby, S. J. *British Atlantic, American Frontier: Spaces of Power in Early Modern British America*. Hanover: University Press of New England, 2005.

Hume, D. "Of Refinement of the Arts." In *Political Discourses*. London, 1752.

Hurk, J. "Plan versus Execution: The 'Ideal City' of New Amsterdam: Seventeenth-Century Netherlandic Town Planning in North America." *New York History* 96, nos. 3–4 (2015), 265–283.

Ingram, D. *Indians and British Outposts in Eighteenth-Century America*. Gainesville: University Press of Florida, 2021.

Ipsen, P. *Daughter of the Trade: Atlantic Slavers and Interracial Marriage on the Gold Coast*. Philadelphia: University of Pennsylvania Press, 2015.

Johnson, D. *Occupied America: British Military Rule and the Experience of Revolution*. Philadelphia: University of Pennsylvania Press, 2020.

Johnson, J. M. *Wicked Flesh: Black Women, Intimacy, and Freedom in the Atlantic World*. Philadelphia: University of Pennsylvania Press, 2020.

Johnson, L. *Workshop of Revolution: Plebeian Buenos Aires and the Atlantic World, 1776–1810*. Durham, NC: Duke University Press, 2011.

Johnson, M. "Denmark Vesey and His Co-conspirators." *The William and Mary Quarterly* 58, no. 4 (2001), 915–976.

Johnson, M. and J. Roark. *Black Masters: A Free Family of Color in the Old South*. New York: W. W. Norton, 1986.

Johnson, R. *Slavery's Metropolis: Unfree Labor in New Orleans during the Age of Revolutions*. Cambridge: Cambridge University Press, 2016.

Johnson, W. *Soul by Soul: Life inside the Antebellum Slave Market*. Cambridge, MA: Harvard University Press, 2009.

Joyce, A. "Theorizing Urbanism in Ancient Mesoamerica." *Ancient MesoAmerica* 20, no. 2 (2009), 189–196.

Kagan, R. *Urban Images of the Hispanic World, 1493–1793*. New Haven, CT: Yale University Press, 2000.

Kea, R. "City-State Culture on the Gold Coast: The Fante City-State Federation in the Seventeenth and Eighteenth Centuries." In *A Comparative Study of Thirty City-State Cultures: An Investigation*, edited by M. H. Hansen, 191–221. Copenhagen: The Royal Danish Academy of Sciences and Letters, 2000.

Kinsbruner, J. *Independence in Spanish America: Civil Wars, Revolutions, and Underdevelopment*. Albuquerque: University of New Mexico Press, 2000.

Klingelhofer, E., ed. *First Forts: Essays on the Archaeology of Proto-colonial Fortifications*. Leiden: Brill, 2012.

Klooster, W. *The Dutch Moment: War, Trade, and Settlement in the Seventeenth-Century Atlantic World*. Ithaca, NY: Cornell University Press, 2016.

Klooster, W. "Introduction: The Rise and Transformation of the Atlantic World." In *The Atlantic World: Essays on Slavery, Migration and*

Imagination, edited by W. Klooster and A. Padula, 1–42. New York: Taylor & Francis, 2005.

Kolata, A. "Mimesis and Monumentalism in Native Andean Cities." *RES: Anthropology and Aesthetics* 29/30 (1996), 223–236.

Kolata, A. *The Tiwanaku: Portrait of an Andean Civilization*. Cambridge: Blackwell, 1993.

Konove, A. *Black Market Capital: Urban Politics and the Shadow Economy in Mexico*. Berkeley: University of California Press, 2018.

Konove, A. "On the Cheap: The Baratillo Marketplace and the Shadow Economy of Eighteenth-Century Mexico City." *The Americas* 72, no. 2 (2015), 249–278.

Kraay, H. *Bahia's Independence: Popular Politics and Patriotic Festival in Salvador, Brazil (1824–1900)*. Montreal: McGill-Queen's University Press, 2019.

Kulstad-González, P. "Striking It Rich in the Americas' First Boom Town: Economic Activity at Concepción de la Vega (Hispaniola) 1495–1564." In *Archaeology of Culture Contact and Colonialism in Spanish and Portuguese America*, edited by P. Funari and M. Senatore, 313–338. New York: Springer, 2015.

Kupperman, K. O. *Roanoke: The Abandoned Colony*. Lanham, MD: Rowman & Littlefield, 2007.

Landers, J. "The African Landscape of Seventeenth-Century Cartagena and Its Hinterlands." In *The Black Urban Atlantic in the Age of the Slave Trade*, edited by J. Cañizares-Esguerra, M. D. Childs, and J. Sidbury, 147–162. Philadelphia: University of Pennsylvania Press, 2013.

Lane, K. E. *Colour of Paradise: The Emerald in the Age of Gunpowder Empires*. New Haven, CT: Yale University Press, 2010.

Lane, K. E. *Potosi: The Silver City That Changed the World*. Berkeley: University of California Press, 2019.

Lepore, J. *New York Burning: Liberty, Slavery, and Conspiracy in Eighteenth-Century Manhattan*. New York: Vintage Books, 2006.

Levy, B. *Town Born: The Political Economy of New England from Its Founding to the Revolution*. Philadelphia: University of Pennsylvania Press, 2011.

Law, R. *Ouidah: The Social History of a West African Slaving "Port", 1727–1892*. Athens: Ohio University Press, 2004.

Lay, S. *The Reconquest Kings of Portugal: Political and Cultural Reorientation on the Medieval Frontier*. New York: Palgrave Macmillan, 2009.

Leite, A. R. "Defender Almas e Corpos nos Açores (1534–1600): arquitetura, urbanismo, e fortificação." In *Martinho Lutero e Portugal: diálogos, tensões, e impactos*, edited by E. M. Albert, A. P. M. Avelar, M. M. S. N. Lalanda, and P. C. Lopes, 321–334. Lisbon: CHAM, 2019.

Léry, J. *Histoire d'un voyage fait en la terre du Brésil*, translated by J. Whatley. Berkeley: University of California Press, 1990.

Levecq, C. *Black Cosmopolitans: Race, Religion, and Republicanism in an Age of Revolution*. Charlottesville: University of Virginia Press, 2019.

Lilley, K. "'Non urbe, non vico, non castris': Territorial Control and the Colonization and Urbanization of Wales and Ireland under Anglo-Norman Lordship." *Journal of Historical Geography* 26, no. 4 (2000), 517–531.

Lilley, K. "Urban Landscapes and the Cultural Politics of Territorial Control in Anglo-Norman England." *Landscape Research* 24 (1999), 5–23.

Lounsbury, C. R. *The Courthouses of Early Virginia: An Architectural History*. Charlottesville: University of Virginia Press, 2005.

Lovejoy, P. *Transformations in Slavery: A History of Slavery in Africa*. New York: Cambridge University Press, 2012.

Mangan, J. *Trading Roles: Gender, Ethnicity, and the Urban Economy in Colonial Potosi*. Durham, NC: Duke University Press, 2005.

Manion, J. *Liberty's Prisoners: Carceral Culture in Early America*. Philadelphia: University of Pennsylvania Press, 2015.

Mann, K. *Slavery and the Birth of an African City: Lagos, 1760–1900*. Bloomington: Indiana University Press, 2007.

Marquez, J. C. "Afflicted Slaves, Faithful Vassals: *Sevícias*, Manumission, and Enslaved Petitioners in Eighteenth-Century Brazil." *Slavery and Abolition* 43, no. 1 (2022), 91–119.

Martinez, J. L. "La Rebelión de Manco Inka Y Vilcabamba en Textos Andinos Coloniales: Otros Materiales para su Estudo." *Boletín del Museu Chileno de Arte Precolombino* 25, no. 1 (2020), 57–80.

Martinez, M. E. "Space, Order, and Group Identities in a Spanish Colonial Town: Puebla de los Angeles." In *The Collective and the Public in Latin America: Cultural Identities and Political Order*, edited by L. Roniger and T. Herzog, 13–36. Eastbourne: Sussex Academic Press, 2000.

Maser, M. "Conquered Cities: Continuity and Transformation of Urban Structures in the Castillian '*Reconquista*' territories (11th–14th Centuries) – Toledo and Seville." In *The Power of Cities: The Iberian Peninsula from Late Antiquity to the Early Modern Period*, edited by S. Panzram, 201–246. Leiden: Brill, 2019.

McAlister, L. N. *Spain and Portugal in the New World*. New York: Oxford University Press, 1984.

McFarlane, A. *Columbia before Independence: Economy, Society, and Politics under Bourbon Rule*. New York: Cambridge University Press, 2002.

McFarlane, A. "Rebellions in Late Colonial Spanish America: A Comparative Perspective." *Bulletin of Latin American Research* 14, no. 3 (1995), 313–338.

Meraglia, S., Angelucci, C., and Voigtländer, N. "How Merchant Towns Shaped Parliaments: From the Norman Conquest of England to the Great Reform Act." Working Paper Series (Cambridge, MA: National Bureau of Economic Research, 2017).

Metcalf, A. *Go-Betweens and the Colonization of Brazil, 1500–1600*. Austin: University of Texas Press, 2005.

Metcalf, A. "The Society of Jesus and the First *Aldeias* of Brazil." In *Native Brazil: Beyond the Convert and the Cannibal, 1500–1900*, edited by H. Langfur, 29–61. Albuquerque: University of New Mexico Press, 2014.

Middleton, S. *From Privileges to Rights: Work and Politics in Colonial New York City*. Philadelphia: University of Pennsylvania Press, 2011.

Middleton, S. "'How It Came That Bakers Bake No Bread': A Struggle for Trade Privileges in Seventeenth-Century New Amsterdam." *The William and Mary Quarterly* 58, no. 2 (2001), 347–372.

Middleton, S. "William Fishbourn's 'Misfortune': Public Accounting and Paper Money in Early Pennsylvania." *Early American Studies: An Interdisciplinary Journal* 19, no. 1 (2021), 64–99.

Milner, G. R. "Palisaded Settlements in Prehistoric Eastern North America." In *City Walls: The Urban Enceinte in Global Perspective*, edited by J. Tracy, 46–70. Cambridge: Cambridge University Press, 2000.

Miranda, F. "Before the Empire: Portugal and the Atlantic Trade in the Late Middle Ages." *Journal of Medieval Iberian Studies* 5, no. 1 (2013), 69–85.

Monroe, J. C. "'Elephants for Want of Towns': Archaeological Perspectives on West African Cities and Their Hinterlands." *Journal of Archaeological Research* 26, no. 4 (2018), 387–446.

Monroe, J. C. "Urbanism on West Africa's Slave Coast: Archaeology Sheds New Light on Cities in the Era of the Atlantic Slave Trade." *American Scientist* 99, no. 5 (2011), 400–409.

Moorhead, M. L. *The Presidio: Bastion of the Spanish Borderlands*. Norman: University of Oklahoma Press, 1975.

Morgan, K. *Bristol and the Atlantic Trade in the Eighteenth Century*. Cambridge: Cambridge University Press, 1993.

Mulcahy, M. "The 'Great Fire' of 1740 and the Politics of Disaster Relief in Colonial Charleston." *The South Carolina Historical Magazine* 99, no. 2 (1998), 135–157.

Mumford, J. *Vertical Empire: The General Resettlement of Indians in the Colonial Andes*. Durham, NC: Duke University Press, 2012.

Mundy, B. E. *The Death of Aztec Tenochtitlan, the Life of Mexico City*. Austin: University of Texas Press, 2015.

Murillo, D. V. *Urban Indians in a Silver City: Zacatecas, Mexico, 1546–1810*. Stanford, CA: Stanford University Press, 2016.

Musselwhite, P. *Urban Dreams, Rural Commonwealth: The Rise of Plantation Society in the Chesapeake*. Chicago, IL: University of Chicago Press, 2019.

Nash, G. *Forging Freedom: The Formation of Philadelphia's Black Community, 1720–1840*. Cambridge, MA: Harvard University Press, 1988.

Nash, G. *The Urban Crucible: Social Change, Political Consciousness, and the Origins of the American Revolution*. Cambridge, MA: Harvard University Press, 1979.

Newitt, M. D. D. *A History of Portuguese Overseas Expansion, 1400–1668*. London: Routledge, 2005.

Nightingale, C. *Earthopolis: A Biography of Our Urban Planet*. Cambridge: Cambridge University Press, 2022.

Ogborn, M. "Global Historical Geographies, 1500–1800." In *Modern Historical Geographies*, edited by B. J. Graham and C. Nash, 43–69. Harlow: Longman, 2000.

O'Hara, M. "The Orthodox Underworld of Colonial Mexico." *Colonial Latin American Review* 17, no. 2 (2008), 233–250.

Oliveira, V. "Gender, Foodstuff Production and Trade in Late-Eighteenth Century Luanda." *African Economic History* 43 (2015), 57–81.

Olsen, A. "The Zenger Case Revisited: Satire, Sedition and Political Debate in Eighteenth Century America." *Early American Literature* 35, no. 3 (2000), 223–245.

Olukoju, A. "Nigerian Cities in Historical Perspective." In *Nigerian Cities*, edited by T. Falola and S. Salm, 11–46. Trenton: Africa World Press, 2004.

Olwell, R. *Masters, Slaves and Subjects: The Culture of Power in the South Carolina Low Country, 1740–1790*. Ithaca, NY: Cornell University Press, 1998.

Osorio, A. B. *Inventing Lima: Baroque Modernity in Peru's South Sea Metropolis*. New York: Palgrave Macmillan, 2008.

Owensby, B. P. *Empire of Law and Indian Justice in Colonial Mexico*. Stanford, CA: Stanford University Press, 2008.

Pagden, A. *Lords of All the World: Ideologies of Empire in Spain, Britain, and France, c. 1500–c. 1800*. New Haven: Yale University Press, 1995.

Pargas, D. A. *Freedom Seekers: Fugitive Slaves in North America, 1800–1860*. New York: Cambridge University Press, 2021.

Parker, G. "The Artillery Fortress As an Engine of European Overseas Expansion, 1480–1750." In *City Walls: The Urban Enceinte in Global*

Perspective, edited by J. D. Tracy, 386–416. New York: Cambridge University Press, 2000.

Parkinson, R. *Thirteen Clocks: How Race United the Colonies and Made the Declaration of Independence*. Chapel Hill: University of North Carolina Press, 2021.

Parrott, D. "The Utility of Fortifications in Early Modern Europe: Italian Princes and Their Citadels, 1540–1640." *War in History* 7, no. 2 (2000), 127–153.

Parsons, C. *A Not-So-New World: Empire and Environment in French Colonial America*. Philadelphia: University of Pennsylvania Press, 2018.

Paul, T. "Credit and Ethnicity in the Urban Atlantic World: Scottish Associational Culture in Colonial Philadelphia." *Early American Studies: An Interdisciplinary Journal*, 13, no. 3 (2015), 661–691.

Pearl, C. R. *Conceived in Crisis: The Revolutionary Creation of an American State*. Charlottesville: University of Virginia Press, 2020.

Pedley, M. S. and Edney, M. H. *The History of Cartography, Volume 4: Cartography in the European Enlightenment*. Chicago, IL: University of Chicago Press, 2020.

Pestana, C. G. *The English Conquest of Jamaica: Oliver Cromwell's Bid for Empire*. Cambridge, MA: Harvard University Press, 2017.

Piker, J. A. *Okfuskee: A Creek Indian Town in Colonial America*. Cambridge, MA: Harvard University Press, 2004.

Poole, R. *Peterloo: The English Uprising*. Oxford: Oxford University Press, 2019.

Price, J. "Glasgow, the Tobacco Trade, and the Scottish Customs, 1707–1730: Some Commercial, Administrative and Political Implications of the Union." *The Scottish Historical Review* 63, no. 175 (1984), 1–36.

Price, R. *First-Time: The Historical Vision of an Afro-American People*. Baltimore, MD: Johns Hopkins University Press, 1983.

Price, R., ed. *Maroon Societies: Rebel Slave Communities in the Americas*. Baltimore, MD: Johns Hopkins University Press, 1996.

Ramirez, S. E. *To Feed and to Be Fed: The Cosmological Bases of Authority and Identity in the Andes*. Stanford, CA: Stanford University Press, 2005.

Randall, A. and Charlesworth, A. *Markets, Market Culture and Popular Protest in Eighteenth Century Britain and Ireland*. Liverpool: Liverpool University Press, 1996.

Reis, J. J. *Slave Rebellion in Brazil: The Muslim Uprising of 1835 in Bahia*. Baltimore, MD: Johns Hopkins University, 1993.

Reis, N. G. *Imagens de Vilas e Cidades do Brasil Colonial*. São Paulo: Editora USPIANA, 2000.

Reps, J. *Tidewater Towns: City Planning in Colonial Virginia and Maryland*. Ann Arbor: University of Michigan Press, 1972.

Restall, M. and Asselbergs, F. *Invading Guatemala: Spanish, Nahua, and Maya Accounts of the Conquest Wars*. University Park: Pennsylvania State University Press, 2007.

Ridner, J. *A Town In-Between: Carlisle, Pennsylvania and the Early Mid-Atlantic Interior*. Philadelphia: University of Pennsylvania Press, 2010.

Robertson, J. *Gone Is the Ancient Glory: Spanish Town, Jamaica, 1534–2000*. Kingston, Jamaica: Ian Randle, 2005.

Romero, A. *Paulistas e Emboabas no Coração das Minas: idéias, práticas e imaginário político no século XVIII*. Belo Horizonte: Editora da UFMG, 2008.

Roney, J. C. *Governed by a Spirit of Opposition: The Origins of American Political Practice in Philadelphia*. Baltimore, MD: Johns Hopkins University Press, 2014.

Rubin, J. *Tears of Repentance: Christian Indian Identity and Community in Colonial Southern New England*. Lincoln: University of Nebraska Press, 2013.

Russell-Wood, A. J. R. *The Portuguese Empire, 1415–1808: A World on the Move*. Baltimore, MD: Johns Hopkins University Press, 1998.

Santos, C. M. "Luanda: A Colonial City between Africa and the Atlantic, Seventeenth and Eighteenth Centuries." In *Portuguese Colonial Cities in the Early Modern World*, edited by L. M. Brockey, 249–272. Farnham: Ashgate, 2008.

Sassen, S. "The Global City: Introducing a Concept." *The Brown Journal of World Affairs* 11, no. 2 (2005), 27–43.

Saupin, G. "The Emergence of Port Towns in Pre-colonial Sub-Saharan Africa, 1450–1850: What Kind of Development Did They Entail?" *International Journal of Maritime History* 32, no. 1 (2020), 172–184.

Scanlan, P. X. *Freedom's Debtors: British Antislavery in Sierra Leone in the Age of Revolution*. New Haven, CT: Yale University Press, 2017.

Schneider, E. A. *The Occupation of Havana: War, Trade, and Slavery in the Atlantic World*. Chapel Hill: University of North Carolina Press, 2018.

Schwartz, S. B. "The 'Mocambo': Slave Resistance in Colonial Bahia." *Journal of Social History* 3, no. 4 (1970), 313–333.

Scott, J. *The Common Wind: Afro-American Currents in the Age of the Haitian Revolution*. London: Verso Books, 2018.

Searing, J. F. "The Seven Years' War in West Africa: The End of Company Rule and the Emergence of the Habitants." In *The Seven Years War*, edited by M. Danley and P. Speelman, 263–291. Leiden: Brill, 2012.

Semley, L. *To Be Free and French: Citizenship in France's Atlantic Empire*. New York: Cambridge University Press, 2017.

Sesay, C. "The Dialectic of Representation: Black Freemasonry, the Black Public, and Black Historiography." *Journal of African American Studies* 17, no. 3 (2013), 380–398.

Shannon, T. *Indians and Colonists at the Crossroads of Empire: The Albany Congress of 1754*. Ithaca, NY: Cornell University Press, 2002.

Sharples, J. T. *The World That Fear Made: Slave Revolts and Conspiracy Scares in Early America*. Philadelphia: University of Pennsylvania Press, 2020.

Shumway, R. *The Fante and the Transatlantic Slave Trade*. Rochester, NY: University of Rochester Press, 2011.

Sicking, L. "The Medieval Origin of the Factory or the Institutional Foundations of Overseas Trade: Toward a Model for Global Comparison." *Journal of World History* 31, no. 2 (2020), 295–326.

Sierra Silva, P. *Urban Slavery in Colonial Mexico: Puebla de los Angeles, 1531–1706*. Cambridge: Cambridge University Press, 2018.

Sivasundaram, S., Bashford, A., and Armitage, D. "Introduction: Writing World Oceanic Histories." In *Oceanic Histories*, edited by D. Armitage, A. Bashford, and S. Sivasundaram, 1–28. Cambridge: Cambridge University Press, 2017.

Smallwood, S. *Saltwater Slavery: A Middle Passage from Africa to American Diaspora*. Cambridge, MA: Harvard University Press, 2007.

Smith, M. "Cities in the Aztec Empire: Commerce, Imperialism, and Urbanization." In *Rethinking the Aztec Economy*, edited by D. Nichols, F. Berdan, and M. Smith, 44–67. Tucson: University of Arizona Press, 2017.

Sparks, R. *The Two Princes of Calabar: An Eighteenth-Century Atlantic Odyssey*. Cambridge, MA: Harvard University Press, 2004.

Sparks, R. *Where the Negroes Are Masters: An African Port in the Era of the Slave Trade*. Cambridge, MA: Harvard University Press, 2014.

Spieler, M. "Slave Voice and the Legal Archive: The Case of Freedom Suits before the Paris Admiralty Court." In *Hearing Enslaved Voices: African and Indian Slave Testimony in British and French America, 1700–1848*, edited by S. White and T. Burnard, 165–187. New York: Taylor & Francis, 2020.

Stanley, A. "Praying Indian Towns: Encounter and Conversion through Imposed Urban Spaces." In *Building the British Atlantic World: Spaces, Places, and Material Culture 1600–1850*, edited by D. Maudlin and B. L. Herman, 142–162. Chapel Hill: University of North Carolina Press, 2016.

Subrahmanyam, S. "Introduction." In *The Cambridge World History, Volume 6: The Construction of a Global World, 1400–1800 CE*, edited by J. H. Bentley, S. Subrahmanyam, and M. E. Wiesner-Hanks, 1–26. Cambridge: Cambridge University Press, 2015.

Thornton, J. *A Cultural History of the Atlantic World, 1250–1820*. New York: Cambridge University Press, 2012.

Thornton, J. "Mbanza Kongo/São Salvador: Kongo's Holy City." In *Africa's Urban Past*, edited by D. M. Anderson and R. Rathbone, 67–84. Oxford: James Currey Publishers, 2000.

Townsend, C. *Malintzin's Choices: An Indian Woman in the Conquest of Mexico*. Albuquerque: University of New Mexico Press, 2006.

Tracy, J. D. *City Walls: The Urban Enceinte in Global Perspective*. New York: Cambridge University Press, 2000.

Truxes, T. *Defying Empire: Trading with the Enemy in Colonial New York*. New Haven, CT: Yale University Press, 2008.

Twinam, A. *Purchasing Whiteness: Pardos, Mulattos, and the Quest for Social Mobility in the Spanish Indies*. Stanford, CA: Stanford University Press, 2015.

Tyson, J. "Lady Huntingdon's Reformation." *Church History* 64, no. 4 (1995), 580–593.

Uribe-Uran, V. "The Birth of a Public Sphere in Latin America during the Age of Revolution." *Comparative Studies in Society and History* 42, no. 2 (2000), 425–457.

Usner, D. H. *Indians, Settlers and Slaves in a Frontier Exchange Economy: The Lower Mississippi Valley before 1783*. Chapel Hill: University of North Carolina Press, 1992.

Vagnon, E. "Pluricultural Sources of the Catalan Atlas." In *Cartography between Christian Europe and the Arabic-Islamic World, 1100–1500: Divergent Traditions*, edited by A. Hiatt, 160–188. Leiden: Brill, 2021.

Valdez, L. and Valdez, J. E. "From Rural to Urban: Archaeological Research in the Periphery of Huari, Ayacucho Valley, Peru." *Journal of Anthropology* (2017), https://doi.org/10.1155/2017/3597297.

Van Cleve, G. "Somerset's Case and Its Antecedents in Imperial Perspective." *Law and History Review* 24, no. 3 (Fall 2006), 601–646.

Vidal, L. *Mazagão, la ville qui traversa l'Atlantique du Maroc à l'Amazonie, 1769–1783*. Paris: Aubier, 2005.

Vidal, L. "Une Fondation Atlantique: la *Vila* São Jorge do Rio dos Ilhéus (1535–1548)." In *Les Fondations de Villes sur les Litoraux Américains: Brésil et États-Unis, XVI*^e^*–XIX*^e^ *siècles*, edited by L. Vidal and B. Van Ruymbeke, 31–54. Reines: Les Perséides, 2021.

Vogel, M., Smit, M., Masson, M., and Janusek, J. W. *The Casma City of El Purgatorio: Ancient Urbanism in the Andes*. Gainesville: University Press of Florida, 2016.

Voigt, L. *Spectacular Wealth: The Festivals of Colonial South American Mining Towns*. Austin: University of Texas Press, 2016.

Walker, C. *Smoldering Ashes: Cuzco and the Creation of Republican Peru, 1780–1840*. Durham, NC: Duke University Press, 1999.

Webster, S. "Masters of the Trade: Native Artisans, Guilds, and the Construction of Colonial Quito." *Journal of the Society of Architectural Historians* 68, no. 1 (2009), 10–29.

Wells, A. "Global Cities, Glocal Fauna: Animals and the Urban British Atlantic, 1660–1800." *Urban History* 48, no. 3 (2020), 498–517.

White, S. *Voices of the Enslaved: Love, Labor, and Longing in French Louisiana*. Chapel Hill: University of North Carolina Press, 2019.

Williams, J. S. "The Evolution of the Presidio in Northern New Spain." *Historical Archaeology* 38, no. 3 (2004), 6–23.

Wilson, K. *The Sense of the People: Politics, Culture, and Imperialism in England, 1715–1785*. Cambridge: Cambridge University Press, 1995.

Wilson, K. "Urban Culture and Political Activism in Hanoverian England: The Example of Voluntary Hospitals." In *The Transformation of Political Culture: England and Germany in the Late Eighteenth Century*, edited by E. Hellmuth, 165–184. London: German Historical Institute.

Winters, C. "The Urban Systems of Medieval Mali." *Journal of Historical Geography* 7, no. 4 (1981), 341–355.

Yannakakis, Y. *The Art of Being In-Between: Native Intermediaries, Indian Identity, and Local Rule in Colonial Oaxaca*. Durham, NC: Duke University Press, 2008.

Zabin, S. *Dangerous Economies: Status and Commerce in Imperial New York*. Philadelphia: University of Pennsylvania Press, 2009.

Zahedieh, N. *The Capital and the Colonies: London and the Atlantic Economy, 1660–1700*. Cambridge: Cambridge University Press, 2010.

Cambridge Elements

Global Urban History

About the series

This series proposes a new understanding of urban history by reinterpreting the history of the world's cities. While urban history has tended to produce single-city case studies, global history has mostly been concerned with the interconnectedness of the world. Combining these two approaches produces a new framework to think about the urban past. The individual titles in the series emphasize global, comparative, and transnational approaches. They deliver empirical research about specific cities, while also exploring questions that expand the narrative outside the immediate locale to give insights into global trends and conceptual debates. Authored by established and emerging scholars whose work represents the most exciting new directions in urban history, this series makes pioneering research accessible to specialists and non-specialists alike.

Cambridge Elements

Global Urban History

Elements in the series

How Cities Matter
Richard Harris

Real Estate and Global Urban History
Alexia Yates

Cities and News
Lila Caimari

The Modern City in Asia
Kristin Stapleton

Epidemic Cities
Antonio Carbone

Urban Disasters
Cindy Ermus

Making Cities Socialist
Katherine Zubovich

Early Modern Atlantic Cities
Mariana Dantas and Emma Hart

A full series listing is available at: www.cambridge.org/EGUB

For EU product safety concerns, contact us at Calle de José Abascal, 56–1°,
28003 Madrid, Spain or eugpsr@cambridge.org.

www.ingramcontent.com/pod-product-compliance
Ingram Content Group UK Ltd.
Pitfield, Milton Keynes, MK11 3LW, UK
UKHW022147080726
473066UK00010B/815